IDIOT'S GUIDES.
AS EASY AS IT GETS!

Slow Cooker Cooking

by Rachel Farnsworth

ALPHA

A member of Penguin Group (USA) Inc.

To my grandpa, who taught me to dream big and work hard.
And to Marissa, who taught me to live well and love more.
And to all the people who gather their families around the dinner table each night.
You make the world a better place.

ALPHA BOOKS

Published by Penguin Group (USA) Inc.

Penguin Group (USA) Inc., 375 Hudson Street, New York, New York 10014, USA • Penguin Group (Canada), 90 Eglinton Avenue East, Suite 700, Toronto, Ontario M4P 2Y3, Canada (a division of Pearson Penguin Canada Inc.) • Penguin Books Ltd., 80 Strand, London WC2R 0RL, England • Penguin Ireland, 25 St. Stephen's Green, Dublin 2, Ireland (a division of Penguin Books Ltd.) • Penguin Group (Australia), 250 Camberwell Road, Camberwell, Victoria 3124, Australia (a division of Pearson Australia Group Pty. Ltd.) • Penguin Books India Pvt. Ltd., 11 Community Centre, Panchsheel Park, New Delhi—110 017, India • Penguin Group (NZ), 67 Apollo Drive, Rosedale, North Shore, Auckland 1311, New Zealand (a division of Pearson New Zealand Ltd.) • Penguin Books (South Africa) (Pty.) Ltd., 24 Sturdee Avenue, Rosebank, Johannesburg 2196, South Africa • Penguin Books Ltd., Registered Offices: 80 Strand, London WC2R 0RL, England

IDIOT'S GUIDES and Design are trademarks of Penguin Group (USA) Inc.

International Standard Book Number: 978-1-61564-606-7
Library of Congress Catalog Card Number: 2014933133

16 15 14   8 7 6 5 4 3 2 1

Interpretation of the printing code: The rightmost number of the first series of numbers is the year of the book's printing; the rightmost number of the second series of numbers is the number of the book's printing. For example, a printing code of 14-1 shows that the first printing occurred in 2014.

Note: This publication contains the opinions and ideas of its author. It is intended to provide helpful and informative material on the subject matter covered. It is sold with the understanding that the author and publisher are not engaged in rendering professional services in the book. If the reader requires personal assistance or advice, a competent professional should be consulted. The author and publisher specifically disclaim any responsibility for any liability, loss, or risk, personal or otherwise, which is incurred as a consequence, directly or indirectly, of the use and application of any of the contents of this book.

Most Alpha books are available at special quantity discounts for bulk purchases for sales promotions, premiums, fundraising, or educational use. Special books, or book excerpts, can also be created to fit specific needs. For details, write: Special Markets, Alpha Books, 375 Hudson Street, New York, NY 10014.

Publisher: *Mike Sanders*
Executive Managing Editor: *Billy Fields*
Senior Acquisitions Editor: *Brook Farling*
Development Editorial Supervisor: *Christy Wagner*
Senior Production Editor: *Janette Lynn*
Design Supervisor: *William Thomas*
Indexer: *Johnna VanHoose Dinse*
Layout: *Laura Merriman, Ayanna Lacey*
Proofreader: *Cate Schwenk*

Contents

Introduction

I believe in cooking from scratch with love. Slow cooker cooking is no exception. The recipes in this book are made from scratch wherever possible and plausible. Preparation time has been kept to an absolute minimum to maximize the convenience of the slow cooker but without sacrificing the quality. My culinary endeavors have taken me many places, but I am, first and foremost, a home cook just like you. I know how life goes, and I know exactly why you want to incorporate the slow cooker into your life. This handy appliance is a valuable tool in the kitchen and, when used properly, can produce stunning dishes. Not every dish is best suited for slow cooking, but it's certainly a valid cooking method that can be used for a wide array of dishes to add convenience—and delicious flavor—to your menu.

The more than 150 recipes and variations in this book are designed to showcase the slow cooker's wide range of capabilities while still presenting dishes your family will enjoy. All the photos included with the recipes are photos of the actual finished dish I cooked in my slow cooker. No enhancements or inedible staging techniques were used. No tricks or gimmicks, just real food.

I've included lots of notes and tips throughout the book as well as pointers on ingredients and cooking methods—both for slow cooker cooking and cooking in general. Even if you're an experienced slow cooker cook, it's my hope that you can find new ideas and inspiration in the pages that follow.

Special Thanks to the Technical Reviewer

Idiot's Guides: Slow Cooker Cooking was reviewed by an expert who double-checked the accuracy of what you'll learn here, to help us ensure this book gives you everything you need to know about making delicious dishes in your slow cooker. Special thanks are extended to Trish Sebben-Krupka.

Acknowledgments

This book would not have been possible without my huge support team who has helped me every step of the way. While this book might not be dedicated to him, my life is certainly dedicated to my wonderful husband, Stephen, who supports me in my crazy dreams, late work nights, and culinary successes—and failures. A special thanks to my mother, who coached me with her artistic abilities. I love you, Mom! My children put up with a lot for this book, and I appreciate their patience, independence, and unfeigned love for their mother's cooking. You two are my little sous chefs, and although I could have worked faster and more efficiently without you, there just wouldn't have been as much love in the food. Thank you to the team of taste testers and friends who devoured the food shown in this book. You know who you are. I cannot possibly forget the people who make me look good—my team at Alpha Books, Brook Farling, Christy Wagner, and William Thomas.

Chapter 1

Slow Cooker Fundamentals

Welcome to the world of slow cooking, where the magic of low heat and slow cook times come together to yield flavorful foods you can prepare, put in the slow cooker, and let this handy appliance do the work for you.

This book is full of recipes, tips, and tricks to help you make the most of your slow cooker. In this chapter, you learn how slow cookers work, pick up some food safety essentials, and explore how to troubleshoot any problems you happen to encounter.

How a Slow Cooker Works

Slow cookers come in multiple shapes and sizes. The most common shapes you'll see are oval and round. Oval slow cookers are increasingly popular because they hold odd-shaped roasts with ease. Round slow cookers tend to be deeper and allow ingredients to be stacked.

Slow cooker sizes are measured in quarts. The smallest size available is a 1-quart (1-liter) slow cooker, while the largest slow cookers hold up to 12 quarts (11.5 liters). The recipes in this book are geared toward the most common size range of 6 to 8 quarts (5.5 to 7.5 liters) unless otherwise noted.

Parts of a Slow Cooker

A slow cooker consists of a few basic parts. All slow cookers have a stoneware insert, a heating base unit, and a lid. The stoneware insert is where you place the food. The insert fits inside the heating base unit, which slowly heats up the stoneware. The lid is most commonly made of glass, which allows you to see your food as it cooks so you don't have to remove the lid and let all that precious heat and steam out.

Slow Cooker Settings

Temperature controls are available in several levels of sophistication. Basic slow cookers have one temperature setting, although most slow cookers have three settings: low, high, and warm. More sophisticated slow cookers have digital timers, are programmable, and will automatically switch to the warm setting after the programmed cook time is over. Some slow cookers make the switch to warm without a timer after 8 hours. Check your owner's manual to understand which of these features your slow cooker has.

The settings on a slow cooker refer to the wattage the heating element uses and not necessarily the actual temperature the slow cooker reaches. There's no standard temperature, so there's variation among models.

The ideal temperature range for slow cooking is between 190°F and 210°F (90°C and 100°C). Most slow cookers have a maximum high temperature of 200°F (95°C), but some can reach up to 300°F (150°C). A dish should reach the ideal temperature range within several hours on low and less than an hour on high. On some models, the high setting simply means the machine reaches the temperature faster, while on other models, it means it reaches a higher temperature. Check your owner's manual to learn how hot your slow cooker gets or test it with a thermometer.

The warm setting is designed to keep foods at a consistent food-safe temperature. This needs to be at least 140°F (60°C). Food can be safely held on the warm setting for up to 4 hours.

Unless specifically indicated in the recipe, most foods turn out best if cooked on the low setting. Some foods, particularly meats, can taste watery and "boiled" when cooked on high.

Food Safety

Although the nature of slow cookers means you can prepare your meal, fill the slow cooker, and let it do the work for you, no slow cooker enables you to fill it and set it to turn on at a later time. This would mean your food would set out at room temperature, increasing the possibility of bacterial growth.

A better, safer alternative is to prepare the food, place it in the stoneware vessel, and store the bowl in the refrigerator until you're ready to cook and then cook on the low setting. The slow warming of the stoneware prevents it from cracking or breaking, as might happen if exposed to high heat. Likewise, do not store your stoneware in the freezer or place hot stoneware into the refrigerator or freezer.

The United States Department of Agriculture recommends that meats be cooked to the temperatures given in the following table. Check your country's guidelines for standards in your area.

Food	Minimum Internal Temperature
All poultry	165°F (75°C)
Casseroles	165°F (75°C)
Ground meats	160°F (70°C)
Eggs	160°F (70°C)
Beef, pork, veal, and lamb (steaks, chops, and roasts)	145°F (65°C)
Ham, fresh or smoked (uncooked)	145°F (65°C)
Fish and shellfish	145°F (65°C)
Fully cooked ham (to reheat)	140°F (60°C)

With few exceptions (such as frozen pastas that have already been cooked before being frozen), before you add any food to the slow cooker, it should be completely thawed. Due to the nature of slow cooking, frozen foods won't reach a safe temperature in time to prevent the growth of bacteria.

Don't Be Afraid to Experiment

One of the great things about slow cooker cooking is how much of the work is done for you. You prepare the ingredients, add them to the slow cooker, and the appliance cooks your dish without much, if any, further help from you. Another bonus of slow cooker cooking is how versatile a cooking method it is. Unless a recipe calls for a certain type of apple, onion, milk, or other ingredient, you can use whatever variety, color, or kind you like best.

If you're not sure which to use, try making the recipe with one version first—a Granny Smith apple in your applesauce, a red onion in your stir-fry, or whole milk in your bread pudding. The next time, use different versions—a Honeycrisp apple, a white onion, or skim milk, for example.

Note which variations you like better for the next time you make the recipe—or try something different then, too! Experiment until you find just the right combination of ingredients that makes your mouth water.

Slow Cooker Cleaning and Care

A slow cooker's stoneware vessel and glass lid are often dishwasher safe, but check your owner's manual to see if your particular model is an exception. If they're not, you can wash them by hand using dish soap and hot water.

Stubborn, baked-on messes can be tough to scrub clean. If you notice a baked-on ring has formed in the stoneware vessel, fill the bowl with enough water to cover the ring. Keep the slow cooker on the low setting for 1 or 2 hours, and the ring should be easy to scrub off.

You can remove other spots and stains using baking soda. Make a paste of baking soda and water, and scrub the paste onto the spot. Let sit for 20 minutes, and rinse away the grime.

If the heat base unit becomes dirty, first try cleaning it with a damp cloth. Be careful not to use too much water because the base contains all the electrical parts of the appliance. *Never submerge the base in water.* For particularly stubborn messes, you can try oven cleaner. Be sure to do this in an area with plenty of ventilation, as oven cleaner contains toxic chemicals.

Slow cooker liners can make clean up quick and easy. They are generally sold in the same area of the store as aluminum foil, parchment paper, and plastic storage bags.

Troubleshooting Tips

For best results, and unless the recipe indicates otherwise, keep the lid on your slow cooker as it cooks. Removing the lid allows heat to escape, and it takes 20 to 30 minutes for the slow cooker to get back to the appropriate temperature.

Place ingredients that cook slowest on the bottom of the slow cooker so they have more direct access to the bottom heat source. Vegetables generally cook faster than meats, so place them toward the top of the stoneware vessel unless otherwise noted in the recipe. Root vegetables, like potatoes, are the exception to this rule as, they require longer cook times.

Do not underfill or overfill your slow cooker. A slow cooker should not be less than one third full and not more than three quarters full.

What If the Electricity Goes Out?

If you're home while the slow cooker is cooking and the electricity goes out, keep the lid on. If the power resumes within 30 minutes, you can continue letting your food cook. If the power does not resume within a half hour, you'll either need to find an alternate cooking method or discard the food.

If you discover that the power went out while you were away and don't know how long the electricity was off, it's best to discard food. You can't know for sure how long the food was without heat and potentially subject to bacterial growth.

Why Is My Food Burning?

If you follow a recipe and your food burns, your slow cooker could run hot. You can test the temperature of your cooker by filling it two thirds full of water, turn on the slow cooker, and let it run for 8 hours. After 8 hours, quickly remove the lid and insert an instant-read thermometer in the water to check the temperature.

If you run the test on low, the temperature should read between 190°F (90°C) and 210°F (100°C) after 8 hours. If it's above this temperature, you either need to decrease cook times or purchase a new slow cooker.

If you run the test on high, after 8 hours, the temperature could be anywhere between 190°F (90°C) and 300°F (150°C), although it should be the same temperature range of 190°F (90°C) and 210°F (100°C), as the high setting is normally designed to reach the temperature range faster. Once again, if it's on the higher end of the range, you'll need to either reduce the cooking time or purchase a new slow cooker.

Why Does One Side of My Dish Always Burn?

The side of your slow cooker's heating unit that's opposite the control unit generally tends to run hotter. To lessen this effect, fold a piece of aluminum foil to create a barrier on that side of the slow cooker. You can do the same on any other area that tends to burn. Simply line the foil along the interior of the stoneware insert, and proceed with the recipe as directed. This method is particularly useful with breads and casseroles.

If you prefer not to use aluminum foil, you can rotate the insert halfway through the cooking time to ensure even cooking.

Why Is My Casserole Soggy?

Soggy casseroles are usually the result of using too much liquid. Try decreasing the liquid the next time you make the dish. In the meantime, cook for 30 to 60 minutes on high with the lid off to allow for quick evaporation.

What Are Those Spots on My Stoneware?

Normal wear and tear and even hard water are the most common causes of spots on your stoneware. You can remove many spots and stains via basic cleaning methods, but some simply cannot be removed. Unless these areas affect how your food cooks, they're probably nothing to worry about.

Chapter 2

Good-Morning Breakfasts

Slow cooker breakfasts are so convenient. The general rush of weekday morning routines doesn't leave much time for hot, nutritious breakfasts. Some recipes call for a long enough cook time that you can prepare the dish before bed the night before and wake up to a hot breakfast. Other recipes call for shorter cook times, which enable you to get a few things done before coming back to breakfast. Or perhaps you can utilize the short cook time for nice Sunday brunches. (Remember that food can safely sit on a slow cooker's warm setting for up to 4 hours, in case you want to sleep in.)

In this chapter, I share some fresh takes on breakfast classics and give you everything you need to know to enjoy the most important meal of the day.

Apple-Cinnamon Steel-Cut Oatmeal

Sweet apples and warm cinnamon combine for a flavorful overnight breakfast that utilizes the whole-grain goodness of steel-cut oats. Be prepared to wake up to a house filled with an amazing aroma!

Yield	**5 cups**
Serving Size	**¾ cup**
Prep Time	**5 minutes**
Cook Time	**6 to 8 hours**

1½ cups uncooked steel-cut oats

2½ cups apple juice

1½ cups milk

1 large apple, peeled, cored, and diced

2 TB. brown sugar

1 tsp. ground cinnamon

¼ tsp. salt

1. Grease the stoneware insert of a 2- or 3-quart (2- to 3-liter) slow cooker with shortening or oil, or use nonstick cooking spray.

2. In the slow cooker, combine steel-cut oats, apple juice, milk, apple, brown sugar, cinnamon, and salt.

3. Cover and cook on low for 6 to 8 hours.

Variation: Top the finished oatmeal with raisins, walnuts, pecans, or dried fruit.

This recipe is best made in a 2- or 3-quart (2- to 3-liter) slow cooker because using a larger slow cooker could very likely cause the oatmeal to burn. If you want to use a larger slow cooker, double or triple the recipe to avoid burning. You can then store the leftovers in the refrigerator. Reheat by warming in the microwave on high for 1 minute.

As for what kind of milk and apple to use, take your pick. Any kind of milk, from skim to whole, works well in this recipe, as does your favorite variety of apple.

Who says you can't have dessert for breakfast? In this oatmeal full of chocolaty deliciousness, the sweetness of the brown sugar counteracts the bitterness of the cocoa powder to produce a perfectly chocolate bite with every spoonful.

Yield	5 cups
Serving Size	¾ cup
Prep Time	5 minutes
Cook Time	6 to 8 hours

1½ cups uncooked steel-cut oats

4 cups milk

½ cup cocoa powder

½ cup brown sugar, firmly packed

2 tsp. vanilla extract

1. Grease the stoneware insert of a 2- or 3-quart (2- to 3-liter) slow cooker with shortening or oil, or use nonstick cooking spray.

2. In the slow cooker, combine steel-cut oats, milk, cocoa powder, brown sugar, and vanilla extract.

3. Cover and cook on low for 6 to 8 hours.

Variation: For **German Chocolate Oatmeal,** use 2 cups unsweetened coconut milk instead of regular milk.

When shopping for oats, you're sure to find several different kinds, including steel cut, old fashioned, quick, and instant. Steel-cut oats are the best oats to use in slow cooker recipes. They're whole grain and come from the inner portion of the oat kernel—the oat groats are simply hulled, toasted, and chopped. This minimal processing requires a longer cooking time than old-fashioned, quick, or instant oats, which are progressively more processed. While other oats will become mushy and overcooked in the low, slow heat of a slow cooker, steel-cut oats hold up much better. If you don't have steel-cut oats, you can use rolled oats, but the results will be more porridge-like. Decrease the cooking time to 4 to 6 hours if you opt for rolled oats.

Brownie Batter Oatmeal

Pumpkin Pie Oatmeal

Wake up to the nostalgic and comforting flavors of pumpkin pie with this oatmeal. This recipe embraces the flavors of fall and provides a pleasantly sweet start on those crisp fall mornings.

Yield	5 cups
Serving Size	¾ cup
Prep Time	5 minutes
Cook Time	6 to 8 hours

1 cup uncooked steel-cut oats

4 cups milk

¼ cup brown sugar, firmly packed

1 TB. pumpkin pie spice

1 tsp. vanilla extract

¼ tsp. salt

1 cup pumpkin purée

1. Grease the stoneware insert of a 2- or 3-quart (2- to 3-liter) slow cooker with shortening or oil, or use nonstick cooking spray.

2. In the slow cooker, combine steel-cut oats, milk, brown sugar, pumpkin pie spice, vanilla extract, and salt.

3. Cover and cook on low for 6 to 8 hours.

4. Stir in pumpkin purée when ready to serve.

Variation: You can use 3½ cups almond milk in place of the milk listed here for a vegan version. The almond milk adds a nutty element that complements the flavors of the pumpkin pie.

Pumpkin pie spice is a mixture of cinnamon, nutmeg, ginger, and allspice. You can find it in the spice section of your grocery store. You add the pumpkin purée at the end in order to retain the maximum pumpkin flavor. If you let it stew with the oats in the slow cooker, the flavor will dull and dilute and the texture could become somewhat gritty. Adding it in at the end ensures a fresh, pumpkin flavor.

In this recipe, traditional hashbrowns are loaded with fresh veggies and cheese. The pepper jack, jalapeño, bacon, and bell pepper add Southwestern flair and a little heat to this breakfast favorite.

Yield	6 cups
Serving Size	1 cup
Prep Time	30 minutes
Cook Time	6 to 8 hours

5 strips bacon

3 large russet potatoes, peeled

1 cup milk

¾ cup shredded pepper jack cheese

¾ cup shredded cheddar cheese

1 large red bell pepper, ribs and stems removed, and diced

5 large button mushrooms, sliced

2 TB. sliced green onions

1 jalapeño, stem removed, and diced

½ tsp. salt

¼ tsp. black pepper

1. In a room-temperature skillet over medium heat, cook bacon for 10 minutes. Flip over bacon, and cook for 7 to 10 more minutes or until bacon is crispy. Transfer bacon to a paper towel–covered plate to drain.

2. Meanwhile, using the largest grate on a cheese grater, shred russet potatoes. Squeeze potato shreds to remove any excess water, and place potatoes in a large bowl.

3. To shredded potatoes, add milk, pepper jack cheese, cheddar cheese, red bell pepper, button mushrooms, green onions, jalapeño, salt, and black pepper.

4. Crumble cooked bacon, add to potato bowl, and stir to combine. Scoop mixture into a 4- to 6-quart (4- to 5.5-liter) slow cooker.

5. Cover and cook on low for 6 to 8 hours.

Variation: If you prefer, you can swap out the bacon for 1 pound (450 grams) cooked sausage instead.

Peeled potatoes, and especially peeled and shredded potatoes, start to brown when they're exposed to the air. To prevent this, you need to deprive the potatoes of oxygen. Placing them in a liquid slows the process. In this recipe, for example, you could pour the milk over the shredded potatoes early if you notice they're starting to brown. Also, be careful when working with jalapeños. As you handle them, the jalapeño's oils transfer to your hands, so *do not touch your face or your eyes after cutting a jalapeño!* Wear gloves to prevent the oil transfer, and wash your hands well with dish soap after you're finished handling the pepper to remove the spicy oils from your fingers.

Loaded Hashbrowns

Hearty Sausage and Potato Hash

Flavorful sausage and red potatoes combine for a hearty, savory breakfast that's both filling and satisfying. The juicy sausage drippings create potato bites bursting with bold sausage flavor.

Yield	6 cups
Serving Size	1 cup
Prep Time	10 minutes
Cook Time	5 or 6 hours

12 medium red potatoes (3 lb./1.5kg), chopped into 1-in. (2.5cm) pieces

1 medium yellow onion, diced

½ tsp. salt

¼ tsp. black pepper

¼ tsp. dried oregano

¼ tsp. dried basil

½ cup chicken broth

1 lb. (450g) whole fresh sausage in casings

1. In a 6- to 8-quart (5.5- to 7.5-liter) slow cooker, place red potatoes and yellow onion. Add salt, black pepper, oregano, and basil.

2. Pour in chicken broth, and stir to combine.

3. Place sausage on top of potato mixture.

4. Cover and cook on low for 5 or 6 hours.

5. When ready to serve, remove sausage from the slow cooker and slice into ¼-inch (6.5-millimeter) slices. Return sausage to the slow cooker, stir to combine, and serve hot.

Variation: For a creamy cheesy version, add in 1 cup shredded cheddar cheese and ½ cup milk during the last hour of cooking.

You place the potatoes on the bottom with the sausage on top because meat cooks much faster in the slow cooker than hard root vegetables like potatoes. Placing the potatoes on the bottom gives them more contact with the heating elements and helps them cook quicker. A bonus of this layering is that the cooking process creates savory drippings from the sausage that slowly smother the potatoes with added flavor.

With only six ingredients and a short cooking time, these sweet egg pancakes come together with ease for a filling breakfast or brunch. The edges crisp in the butter for a caramelized, crusty crunch.

Yield	4 slices
Serving Size	1 slice
Prep Time	5 minutes
Cook Time	1 or 2 hours

3 TB. butter, melted

6 large eggs

1 cup all-purpose flour

1 cup milk

1 tsp. vanilla extract

⅛ tsp. salt

1. Pour melted butter into a 6- to 8-quart (5.5- to 7.5-liter) slow cooker.

2. In a large bowl, whisk eggs for 1 minute.

3. Whisk in all-purpose flour, milk, vanilla extract, and salt until well combined and few lumps remain.

4. Pour batter into the buttered slow cooker.

5. Cover and cook on high for 1 or 2 hours or until center is set.

6. Slice and serve topped with a dusting of confectioners' sugar, syrup, or fruit.

Variation: Add 1 teaspoon cinnamon and a dash of nutmeg for a flavor twist.

You may know German pancakes by another name. *Dutch baby, Bismarcks, Dutch puffs,* and *German pancakes* all refer to the same egg-based breakfast popover. When made using more traditional methods, the pancake puffs up and falls before serving. The low heat and large pancake size isn't conducive to the impressive puff. Have no fear though, because the end result is very much the same—and tastes fantastic.

German Pancake

Cinnamon Swirl Coffee Cake

Soft and moist with the zing of cinnamon, this coffee cake makes the perfect breakfast treat. The swirling ensures cinnamon flavor in every bite without being overly sweet.

Yield	10 slices
Serving Size	1 slice
Prep Time	10 minutes
Cook Time	2½ to 3 hours

¾ cup butter, softened

1¾ cups sugar

3 large eggs

1 tsp. vanilla extract

2½ cups all-purpose flour

1 tsp. baking soda

1 tsp. baking powder

1 cup sour cream

1 TB. ground cinnamon

1. Grease the stoneware insert of a 6- to 8-quart (5.5- to 7.5-liter) slow cooker with shortening, or use nonstick cooking spray.

2. In a large bowl, and using an electric mixer on high speed, beat butter and 1½ cups sugar for 2 minutes or until mixture is light and fluffy.

3. Add eggs, and continue to beat with the mixer for about 60 seconds or until blended.

4. Using a rubber spatula, stir in vanilla extract, all purpose flour, baking soda, baking powder, and sour cream. Continue to stir by hand for about 1 minute or until last of flour is incorporated. Batter will be very thick.

5. Spoon half of batter into the slow cooker, and spread to cover the bottom of the stoneware insert.

6. In a small bowl, combine remaining ¼ cup sugar with cinnamon. Sprinkle mixture over batter in the slow cooker.

7. Spoon remaining batter over cinnamon mixture, spreading it out as much as possible. Insert a butter knife into batter, and move it around in a swirling motion or figure-eight pattern to swirl cinnamon sugar into batter. Change the direction of your pattern to ensure all of batter gets swirled. Continue swirling for 60 seconds.

8. Cover and cook on high for 2½ to 3 hours or until a toothpick or knife inserted into middle of cake comes out clean.

9. Invert cake onto a serving platter, and either serve immediately or let cool.

Coffee cakes are meant to be served with coffee, rather than contain coffee as an ingredient. Or perhaps it's just an excuse to have cake for breakfast!

As this casserole cooks, the promise of cinnamon-sugar and vanilla-soaked bread beckons you to the kitchen. The caramelized edges provide a special crispy treat.

Yield	8 slices
Serving Size	1 slice
Prep Time	10 minutes
Cook Time	6 hours

1 (16-oz.; 450g) loaf French bread, cut or torn into 1-in. (2.5cm) cubes

8 oz. (225g) cream cheese, diced

1 cup milk chocolate chips

2½ cups milk

7 large eggs

1 cup heavy cream

½ cup brown sugar, firmly packed

2 tsp. vanilla extract

2 tsp. ground cinnamon

4 TB. butter, softened

1. In a 6- to 8-quart (5.5- to 7.5-liter) slow cooker, toss French bread cubes, cream cheese pieces, and milk chocolate chips.

2. In a large bowl, whisk together milk, eggs, and heavy cream for about 2 minutes or until eggs are incorporated.

3. Add ¼ cup brown sugar, vanilla extract, and cinnamon to egg mixture, and whisk for 30 seconds.

4. Pour egg mixture over bread in the slow cooker.

5. In a small bowl, stir together remaining ¼ cup brown sugar and butter until a crumbly mixture forms. Sprinkle crumble over bread in the slow cooker.

6. Cover and cook on low for 6 hours.

7. Serve plain or topped with your favorite syrup.

Variation: For a fall-inspired **Pumpkin French Toast Casserole,** omit the chocolate chips and add 1 cup pumpkin purée with the milk, eggs, and heavy cream.

You can make French toast with a variety of breads. Some prefer a French bread loaf, while others prefer a challah loaf or brioche. You also can try using sourdough or croissants. Each type of bread produces a slightly different taste and texture.

If you want a less crispy crust for your casserole, use an aluminum foil barrier.

French Toast Casserole

Mexican Breakfast Casserole

This savory breakfast casserole is bursting with flavor. The green chiles, chili powder, crushed red pepper flakes, and pepper jack cheese combine for a mild spice and bold flavor that both wakes you up and fills you up.

Yield	2 cups
Serving Size	1 cup
Prep Time	20 minutes
Cook Time	6 to 8 hours

1 lb. (450g) fully cooked Mexican chorizo sausage, diced

1 (4-oz.; 110g) can diced green chiles, drained

1 medium white or yellow onion, diced

1 large red bell pepper, ribs and seeds removed, and diced

1 cup frozen corn kernels, thawed

10 large eggs

2 cups half-and-half

3 cloves garlic, crushed

2 tsp. chili powder

1/2 tsp. crushed red pepper flakes

1/2 tsp. salt

1/2 tsp. black pepper

1 1/2 cups shredded pepper jack cheese

1 1/2 cups shredded cheddar cheese

20 (5 1/2-in./14cm) corn tortillas

1. In a large bowl, stir together Mexican chorizo sausage, green chiles, white onion, red bell pepper, and corn.

2. In a separate large bowl, whisk together eggs, half-and-half, garlic, chili powder, crushed red pepper flakes, salt, and black pepper.

3. In a medium bowl, combine pepper jack cheese and cheddar cheese.

4. Grease a 6- to 8-quart (5.5- to 7.5-liter) slow cooker with butter or shortening, or use nonstick cooking spray.

5. Cover the bottom of the slow cooker with 5 corn tortillas, tearing tortillas to make them fit, if necessary, so they cover the entire bottom of the stoneware insert. Spoon 1/3 of sausage-vegetable mixture onto tortillas. Top with 1 3/4 cups egg mixture. Finish off with 2/3 cup cheese mixture. Repeat layering to create three layers. Top with a fourth layer of tortillas and remaining 1 cup cheese mixture.

6. Cover and cook on low for 8 hours.

Chorizo is a spicy sausage. The Mexican variation of chorizo uses chile peppers and vinegar to create that spicy zing. If you can't find Mexican chorizo or Spanish chorizo in your grocery store, you can use any spicy sausage as a substitute.

The green kale and red sun-dried tomatoes provide a stunning visual appeal that matches the bold, bright flavors of this frittata. The combination of cheeses adds a sharp richness.

Yield	2 cups
Serving Size	1 cup
Prep Time	15 minutes
Cook Time	8 hours

1 lb. (450g) ground
pork sausage

1 bunch kale, roughly chopped
into 1-in. (2.5cm) pieces

10 large eggs

2 TB. milk

1 cup shredded
provolone cheese

½ cup shredded
mozzarella cheese

¼ cup grated Parmesan cheese

½ cup sun-dried tomatoes,
roughly chopped

1. In a large skillet over medium-high heat, cook pork sausage for about 6 to 8 minutes or until browned.

2. Add kale, turn off heat, cover with a lid or aluminum foil, and let sit for 3 minutes.

3. Meanwhile, in a large bowl, whisk eggs and milk until well combined.

4. Stir in provolone cheese, mozzarella cheese, Parmesan cheese, and sun-dried tomatoes.

5. Stir sausage and kale into egg mixture, and pour resulting mixture into a 6- to 8-quart (5.5- to 7.5-liter) slow cooker.

6. Cover and cook on low for 8 hours.

Variation: You can easily switch up the cheese combinations in this recipe. Try Gruyère, goat cheese, and Parmesan; Gouda, sharp cheddar, and mozzarella; or provolone, Brie, and goat cheese.

Kale is a tough, bitter leafy green that's chock full of vitamins and nutrients. In this recipe, the leaves are placed in with the sausage to steam a bit before they're add to the slow cooker. The steam helps soften the leaves to make them more palatable in the finished frittata.

Triple Cheese Sausage and Kale Frittata

Denver Omelet

Take breakfast back to a Colorado chuck wagon with the classic flavors of this omelet. The hashbrown crust adds a crunchy, filling bottom to the traditional ham, pepper, and onion–filled cheddar omelet.

Yield	6 cups
Serving Size	1 cup
Prep Time	10 minutes
Cook Time	8 hours

1 medium russet potato, peeled

12 large eggs

1 cup milk

1 small yellow onion, diced

1 large green bell pepper, ribs and seeds removed, and diced

1 cup cooked ham, diced

1 cup shredded cheddar cheese

¼ tsp. salt

⅛ tsp. black pepper

1. Using the largest grate on a cheese grater, shred russet potato. Squeeze out excess liquid, and place potatoes in a 6- to 8-quart (5.5- to 7.5-liter) slow cooker.

2. In a large bowl, whisk together eggs and milk until well combined.

3. Stir in yellow onion, green bell pepper, ham, cheddar cheese, salt, and black pepper.

4. Pour mixture into the slow cooker.

5. Cover and cook on low for 8 hours.

What's the difference between omelets, frittatas, and quiches in slow cooking? Aren't they all the same thing? They are all egg-based, but the difference comes in the ratio of eggs to liquid, which results in different consistencies. In this omelet recipe, there's slightly more than 1 tablespoon milk per egg. Frittatas have little, if any, added liquid. Quiches are richer and contain the highest amount of liquid-to-egg ratio.

In this savory quiche, the feta and Parmesan cheeses create a sharp bite to the eggs with just a hint of garlic. The slow cooking process leaves the quiche tender and moist on the inside, with a thin, crisp outer layer.

Yield	8 slices
Serving Size	1 slice
Prep Time	5 minutes
Cook Time	6 to 8 hours

8 large eggs

2 cups milk

2 cups fresh spinach leaves, loosely packed

2 cloves garlic, crushed

¾ cup crumbled feta cheese

½ cup grated Parmesan cheese

¼ tsp. salt

¼ cup shredded mozzarella cheese

1. In a large bowl, whisk together eggs and milk until well combined.

2. Stir in spinach leaves, garlic, feta cheese, Parmesan cheese, and salt.

3. Pour mixture directly into a 6- to 8-quart (5.5- to 7.5-liter) slow cooker, and top with mozzarella cheese.

4. Cover and cook on low for 6 to 8 hours.

Variation: Create a crust using thinly sliced potatoes (⅛ inch/ 3 millimeters thick). Overlap the slices slightly to cover the bottom and line 2 inches (5 centimeters) up the sides of the stoneware. The potatoes will get nice and crispy and give you a crunchy crust to your quiche.

Quiche can be stored and reheated easily. Store in an airtight container in the refrigerator, and reheat in a microwave on high or in a 350°F (180°C) oven for about 10 minutes.

Spinach and Feta Quiche

Ham and Swiss Quiche

Don't be fooled by the simplicity of this recipe. The mild, nutty taste of the cheese melts in with the creamy eggs, while the salty ham balances out the decadence of the custardlike egg dish.

Yield	8 slices
Serving Size	1 slice
Prep Time	10 minutes
Cook Time	8 hours

8 large eggs

2 cups milk

1 small yellow onion, diced

1 cup cooked ham steak, diced

1 cup shredded Swiss cheese

½ tsp. salt

¼ tsp. black pepper

1. In a large bowl, whisk together eggs and milk until well combined.
2. Stir in yellow onion, ham steak, Swiss cheese, salt, and black pepper.
3. Pour mixture into the a 6- to 8-quart (5.5- to 7.5-liter) slow cooker.
4. Cover and cook on low for 8 hours.

Variation: Ham and Swiss is a classic combination, but feel free to try different combinations of meat and cheese with this recipe. Bacon and cheddar, diced chicken and blue cheese, sausage and pepper jack, or pancetta and Gruyère are just a few ideas.

Ham steak is a cooked slice of whole ham sold in the meat department of many grocery stores. You can also use leftover ham or thick-sliced deli ham if you like.

Chapter 3

Dips, Snacks, and More

Slow cookers aren't just limited to meals. They also can be a handy helper for parties when you prepare dishes several hours in advance and let your slow cooker do the work as you visit with your guests. The food can even sit on warm during the party, ensuring hot food for hours.

Low and slow also produces some great snacks and other delights you might be surprised to find made in a slow cooker. Homemade yogurt and applesauce, for example, become a simple task.

In this chapter, you see varying sizes of slow cookers listed because dips and appetizers tend to be made in smaller amounts.

This classic dip, with the creamy mix of artichoke hearts and spinach, is always a party favorite. Basil and garlic add subtle flavoring to enhance the mild taste of the artichokes.

Yield	4 cups
Serving Size	¼ cup
Prep Time	5 minutes
Cook Time	2 or 3 hours

8 oz. (225g) cream cheese

¼ cup mayonnaise

½ cup grated Parmesan cheese

1 clove garlic, crushed

½ tsp. dried basil

¼ tsp. salt

¼ tsp. black pepper

1 (14-oz.; 400g) jar artichoke hearts, drained, and roughly chopped

10 oz. (285g) frozen spinach, thawed and drained

¾ cup shredded mozzarella cheese

1. Lightly grease the stoneware insert of a 2- or 3-quart (2- to 3-liter) slow cooker with butter, shortening, or vegetable oil, or use nonstick cooking spray.

2. In a large bowl, combine cream cheese, mayonnaise, Parmesan cheese, garlic, basil, salt, black pepper, artichoke hearts, spinach, and ½ cup mozzarella cheese.

3. Spread mixture in the slow cooker, and top with remaining ¼ cup mozzarella cheese.

4. Cover and cook on high for 2 or 3 hours.

5. Serve hot with bread or tortilla chips. Store in an airtight container in the refrigerator.

Variation: For a flavor boost, add 5 ounces (140 grams) chopped sun-dried tomatoes with the artichoke hearts.

Excess water can make the dip quite runny, so it's important to thaw and drain the spinach well. You can easily thaw frozen spinach in the microwave. Simply heat on high for 1 minute, stir, and repeat until the spinach is completely thawed. Use your hands to squeeze the spinach, letting all the water drain out.

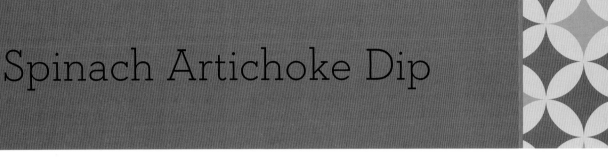

Spinach Artichoke Dip

Southwestern Cheesy Corn Dip

Sweet red bell pepper and corn are given a hint of heat with jalapeño in this creamy corn salsa. Served hot as a dip, it makes for a fun appetizer with southwestern pizzazz.

Yield	3 cups
Serving Size	¼ cup
Prep Time	5 minutes
Cook Time	2 or 3 hours

1 TB. butter, melted

2 cups frozen corn kernels, thawed

½ small yellow onion, diced

1 large red bell pepper, ribs and seeds removed, and diced

2 green onions, green parts only, sliced

1 jalapeño, ribs and seeds removed, and finely diced

1 clove garlic, crushed

¼ cup mayonnaise

½ cup shredded Monterey jack cheese

½ cup shredded cheddar cheese

1. Lightly grease the stoneware insert of a 2- or 3-quart (2- to 3-liter) slow cooker with butter, shortening, or vegetable oil, or use nonstick cooking spray.

2. In a large bowl, stir together melted butter, corn, yellow onion, red bell pepper, green onions, jalapeño, garlic, mayonnaise, Monterey jack cheese, and cheddar cheese.

3. Spread mixture in the slow cooker.

4. Cover and cook on high for 2 or 3 hours.

5. Serve hot with tortilla chips or sliced bread. Store in an airtight container in the refrigerator.

Variation: You can add multiple jalapeños to increase the spiciness of this dip, or substitute a hotter pepper like a serrano.

Green onions are also known as scallions. They have long, tubular green leaves with a white, edible base and are sold in bunches. To clean, remove the bands holding the bunch together and discard any wilted leaves. Using a sharp knife, trim off the stringy roots, and slice the onions about ⅛ inch (3 millimeters) thick. Both the green parts and the white parts are edible and can be used. Your recipe should specify which, but if not, feel free to use both white and green parts.

The spicy kick of buffalo chicken wings is transformed into a convenient dip, complete with chicken, hot sauce, and blue cheese dressing. The cream cheese, cheddar, and ranch dressing give a cool, rich, velvety feel.

Yield	4 cups
Serving Size	¼ cup
Prep Time	5 minutes
Cook Time	6 hours

2 lb. (1kg) boneless, skinless chicken breasts, trimmed

1½ cups buffalo wing sauce

16 oz. (450g) cream cheese

½ cup blue cheese dressing

½ cup ranch dressing

2 cups shredded cheddar cheese

1. In a 2- or 3-quart (2- to 3-liter) slow cooker, add chicken breasts and pour 1 cup buffalo wing sauce over top.

2. Cover and cook on high for 4 hours.

3. Use a fork to shred chicken and then drain any excess liquid from the stoneware insert.

4. Stir in cream cheese, blue cheese dressing, ranch dressing, and cheddar cheese.

5. Cover and cook on high for 2 more hours.

6. Serve hot with tortilla chips, sliced baguettes, carrot sticks, or celery sticks.

If you're short on time, you can use canned chicken in place of the fresh chicken breasts. Use 2 (10-ounce; 285-gram) cans chicken, drained, to replace the fresh chicken. Skip the precooking in steps 1 and 2, add the canned chicken to the slow cooker with the cheese and dressings in step 4, and cook for 2 hours on high.

Buffalo Chicken Dip

Chile Con Queso

Warm, gooey, and with a kick of heat, this Mexican bean dip is packed full of flavor. A bowlful is simple yet satisfying with bites of cheesy beans, bell peppers, and onion.

Yield	6 cups
Serving Size	½ cup
Prep Time	10 minutes
Cook Time	5 hours

1 (15-oz.; 420g) can black beans, drained and rinsed

1 (15-oz.; 420g) can kidney beans, drained and rinsed

1 (15-oz.; 420g) can diced tomatoes, drained

1 (4-oz.; 110g) can diced green chiles, drained

1 (6-oz.; 170g) can tomato paste

2 large red bell peppers, ribs and seeds removed, and diced

1 large yellow onion, diced

4 cloves garlic, crushed

1 TB. chili powder

2½ cups shredded cheddar cheese

8 oz. (225g) cream cheese

1. Lightly grease the stoneware insert of a 4- to 6-quart (4- to 5.5-liter) slow cooker with butter, shortening, or vegetable oil, or use nonstick cooking spray.

2. In the slow cooker, combine black beans, kidney beans, tomatoes, green chiles, tomato paste, red bell peppers, yellow onion, garlic, and chili powder.

3. Cover and cook on high for 4 hours.

4. Stir in cheddar cheese and cream cheese.

5. Cover and cook on high for 1 more hour.

6. Stir before serving hot with tortilla chips.

Variation: Add in a minced jalapeño or serrano pepper to increase the spice level.

Chile con queso translates to "chile with cheese." The dish originates in northern Mexico and has made its way into the heart of Tex-Mex cuisine. It's most often eaten as a dip, but it also can be used as a condiment for quesadillas, tacos, burritos, and enchiladas. This particular recipe is quite hearty, thanks to the vegetables and beans, making it almost a meal unto itself.

Sweet roasted red bell peppers are the star of this creamy dip. Parmesan cheese adds a slight sharpness, and paprika enhances the flavors of the bell peppers.

Yield	3 cups
Serving Size	¼ cup
Prep Time	5 minutes
Cook Time	2 or 3 hours

2 (12-oz.; 340g) jars roasted red bell peppers, drained and roughly chopped

½ cup shredded Parmesan cheese

1 cup shredded mozzarella cheese

8 oz. (225g) cream cheese

2 tsp. ground paprika

2 cloves garlic, peeled and crushed

1. Lightly grease the stoneware insert of a 2- or 3-quart (2- to 3-liter) slow cooker with butter, shortening, or vegetable oil, or use nonstick cooking spray.

2. Thoroughly drain red bell peppers and place in the slow cooker.

3. Stir in Parmesan cheese, mozzarella cheese, cream cheese, paprika, and garlic.

4. Cover and cook on high for 2 or 3 hours.

5. Serve hot with bread or tortilla chips.

Paprika is created by grinding red bell peppers and chile peppers, making it the perfect addition to dishes focused on red bell peppers. You might think paprika doesn't taste particularly good on its own, but adding it to recipes helps bring out the natural sweet and slightly spicy flavors of the bell peppers. Many grocery stores sell paprika labeled as simply "paprika" or "ground paprika." You might also be able to find "sweet paprika" or "smoked paprika." The differences come from the preparation of the peppers and result in subtle variations in intensity and sweetness.

Roasted Red Pepper Dip

Baba Ghanoush

This Middle Eastern dish combines the creamy texture of eggplant, the sweet flavors of roasted garlic, and the nutty flavors sesame seeds in the tahini paste. Lemon juice adds a tangy brightness to this flavorful dip or spread.

Yield	2 cups
Serving Size	¼ cup
Prep Time	5 minutes
Cook Time	2 or 3 hours

1 large eggplant

1 head garlic

1 TB. olive oil

Juice of 1 medium lemon

¼ cup tahini paste

½ tsp. salt

2 TB. fresh parsley, chopped

1. Using a fork, pierce outside of eggplant. Create at least a dozen marks spread out across entire eggplant. Place eggplant in a 4- to 6-quart (4- to 5.5-liter) slow cooker.

2. Cut pointed end off head of garlic, exposing cloves. Drizzle with olive oil, and wrap in aluminum foil. Place wrapped garlic in the slow cooker.

3. Cover and cook on high for 2 or 3 hours.

4. Remove eggplant and garlic from the slow cooker. Cut eggplant in half lengthwise, and use a large spoon to scoop out flesh and place in the bowl of a food processor fitted with an S blade or a blender.

5. Gently squeeze garlic cloves out of their peels and into the food processor or blender.

6. Add lemon juice, tahini paste, and salt, and purée for about 1 minute or until smooth.

7. Refrigerate for 2 hours.

8. Sprinkle with parsley and serve cold with pita chips or pita bread.

The garlic in this recipe is roasted whole. You can use this same method to roast multiple heads of garlic to bring out the sweetness. To substitute roasted garlic in a recipe that calls for raw, double or triple the amount of garlic called for and replace it with roasted.

Variation: For a Mediterranean twist, add ¼ cup chopped sun-dried tomatoes or ¼ cup chopped black olives. Or for an Egyptian version, add 1 diced medium tomato, ½ cup diced white onion, ½ teaspoon cumin, and ½ teaspoon chili powder.

Here, pieces of hearty bread or crisp vegetables are dunked in melted cheese for an ooey-gooey culinary experience.

Yield	1 cup
Serving Size	¼ cup
Prep Time	5 minutes
Cook Time	1½ to 2 hours

¼ cup shredded cheddar cheese

¼ cup shredded Swiss cheese

5 oz. (140g) plain goat cheese

¼ cup white wine

⅛ tsp. ground nutmeg

1. In a 1- or 2-quart (1- to 2-liter) slow cooker, stir together cheddar cheese, Swiss cheese, goat cheese, white wine, and nutmeg.

2. Cover and cook on low for 1½ to 2 hours or until cheeses are melted.

3. Immediately reduce heat to warm, and keep on warm while serving with dipping items such as bread or vegetables.

Variation: Any melting cheese works in this recipe. Feel free to substitute ¼ cup each of three of your favorite cheeses with ¼ cup liquid.

Alcohol does not burn off in slow cooking, so if you need a kid-friendly or alcohol-free version of this dish, a great substitute for the white wine here, or in almost any other recipe, is grape or apple juice.

Cheese Fondue

Homemade Yogurt

Making your own yogurt is easy in a slow cooker. Enjoy the creamy goodness of homemade yogurt—and have fun creating your own flavored versions!

Yield	6 cups
Serving Size	½ cup
Prep Time	5 minutes
Cook Time	8 hours

8 cups whole milk

½ cup plain yogurt with live cultures

1. In a 6- to 8-quart (5.5- to 7.5-liter) slow cooker, add whole milk.

2. Cover and cook on high for 1 hour.

3. Unplug the slow cooker, and let sit, covered, for 30 minutes.

4. Stir in yogurt.

5. Cover, wrap the entire slow cooker in a large bath or beach towel, and let sit undisturbed for 8 to 12 hours.

6. Remove towel, and either refrigerate yogurt as is, or strain yogurt through cheesecloth to remove whey.

7. Store in an airtight container in the refrigerator.

Variation: For **Homemade Vanilla Yogurt,** stir in ¼ cup sugar, honey, or another sweetener, and 2 teaspoons vanilla extract. You also can add mashed fruits for different flavored fruit yogurt.

Yogurt is a fermented milk product. The milk is first heated to about 180°F (80°C) to kill any bacteria already in the milk and then cooled to introduce the bacteria that will ferment into yogurt.

Using a store-bought yogurt is the simplest way to gain a starter. Check the ingredient list before you buy to ensure the yogurt contains live cultures. Those cultures are your starter. For future batches, simply save ½ cup to use as a starter. You can use the last ½ cup left over or store the starter separately in an airtight container in the refrigerator. Homemade yogurt will stay good for about a month when stored this way.

Homemade yogurt is runnier than store-bought varieties. This extra liquid is called whey. You can strain the yogurt through cheesecloth to remove some of the whey. Greek yogurt is strained multiple times to maximize the whey removal. That's why it's so thick.

Traditional applesauce is given a rich, dark color and flavor with the additions of cinnamon and brown sugar for a delectably sweet spiced apple purée.

Yield	6 cups
Serving Size	½ cup
Prep Time	30 minutes
Cook Time	8 hours

5 lb. (2.5kg) apples, peeled, cored, and sliced

½ cup apple juice

½ cup brown sugar, firmly packed

1 TB. ground cinnamon

½ tsp. ground cloves

½ tsp. ground nutmeg

1. In a 6- to 8-quart (5.5- to 7.5-liter) slow cooker, layer apple slices.

2. Pour in apple juice and stir in brown sugar, cinnamon, cloves, and nutmeg.

3. Cover and cook on low for 8 hours.

4. Using a potato masher, mash any remaining apple chunks for a chunky-style applesauce, or transfer to a blender or a food processor fitted with an S blade to purée until smooth.

Variation: For a plain, sugar-free applesauce, substitute water for the apple juice, and omit the brown sugar and spices.

An apple peeler/corer/slicer makes prepping apples quick and easy. If you don't have one, you can use a vegetable peeler to peel the apples and then core and slice them using a knife.

Old-Fashioned Cinnamon Brown Sugar Applesauce

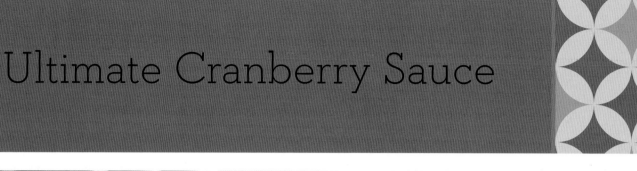

Ultimate Cranberry Sauce

In this delicious and delightful cranberry sauce, the sweetness of the sugars combines with the tartness of the cranberries to produce a sauce with zing. The orange juice provides a punch of citrus to balance it out.

Yield	2 cups
Serving Size	¼ cup
Prep Time	5 minutes
Cook Time	2 hours

3 cups fresh cranberries

½ cup orange juice

½ cup brown sugar, firmly packed

½ cup granulated sugar

1. In a 2- to 4-quart (2- to 4-liter) slow cooker, combine cranberries, orange juice, brown sugar, and granulated sugar.

2. Cover and cook on high for 2 hours.

3. Transfer cranberry sauce to a blender or a food processor fitted with an S blade, and purée until smooth.

4. Serve hot or cold. Store in an airtight container in the refrigerator.

Variation: For a spicy twist on the classic sweet cranberry sauce, add 1 jalapeño, ribs and seeds removed, and diced. Or add 2 cups raspberries for a double berry sauce.

Fresh, homemade cranberry sauce can be served as a sauce on turkey, ham, chicken, or even beef. Cranberries are harvested during the fall months in North America. From September to November, the fields are flooded, and special harvesters knock the berries loose. The cranberries then float to the top of the water and are skimmed or pumped out. Fresh cranberries should be firm or hard. If you find any soft ones in the batch, discard them.

Enjoy the sweet berry goodness of your own fresh, homemade, strawberry jam. Spread it on toast and bagels, or use it to create your lunchtime peanut butter and jelly sandwich. Homemade jam is an absolute treat.

Yield	6 cups
Serving Size	2 tablespoons
Prep Time	30 minutes
Cook Time	6 to 8 hours

4 lb. (2kg) fresh strawberries, hulled and sliced

2 TB. lemon juice

6 cups sugar

4½ TB. pectin

1. In a 6- to 8-quart (5.5- to 7.5-liter) slow cooker, add strawberries, lemon juice, sugar, and pectin.

2. Cover and cook on low for 6 to 8 hours.

3. Using a potato masher, mash strawberries for a chunky jam. Or transfer in batches to a blender or a food processor fitted with an S blade to purée for a smooth jam.

4. Store in an airtight container in the refrigerator for up to 1 month.

Variation: For **Homemade Apricot Jam,** use 4 pounds (2 kilograms) apricots, pitted, peeled, and sliced; ¼ cup lemon juice; 4 cups sugar; and 4½ tablespoons pectin. For **Homemade Peach Jam,** use 4 pounds (2 kilograms) peaches, peeled; ¼ cup lemon juice; 4 cups sugar; and 4½ tablespoons pectin. For **Homemade Blackberry Jam,** use 4 cups blackberries, 2 tablespoons lemon juice, 5 cups sugar, and 4½ tablespoons pectin. For **Homemade Raspberry Jam,** use 4 cups raspberries, 2 tablespoons lemon juice, 5 cups sugar, and 4½ tablespoons pectin.

Pectin is a natural thickening agent. You can find it in almost any grocery store in the baking or canning aisle. Old-fashioned jam recipes did not include pectin, and they were much thinner as a result. Modern jams are more easy to spread due to the thickening power of pectin.

For future use, you can freeze the jam in resealable plastic freezer bags and store for up to 6 to 9 months. Or can the jam using traditional pressure canning methods.

Homemade Strawberry Jam

Apple-Pumpkin Butter

In this sweet, spiced, and condensed butter, the apples and pumpkins reduce, and the flavors concentrate to produce a powerful flavor combination, complete with cinnamon, cloves, nutmeg, and ginger.

Yield	6 cups
Serving Size	2 tablespoons
Prep Time	30 minutes
Cook Time	8 hours

5 lb. (2.5kg) apples, peeled, cored, and sliced

2 cups pumpkin purée

¼ cup apple juice

Juice of 1 medium lemon

1 cup sugar

2 TB. ground cinnamon

1 tsp. ground cloves

1 tsp. ground nutmeg

1 tsp. ground ginger

1. In a 6- to 8-quart (5.5- to 7.5-liter) slow cooker, add apple slices and pumpkin purée.

2. Pour in apple juice, lemon juice, and sugar, and season with cinnamon, cloves, nutmeg, and ginger. Stir well to combine.

3. Cover and cook on low for 8 hours.

4. Transfer apple-pumpkin butter to a blender or a food processor fitted with an S blade, and purée for 1 minute or until smooth. Or use an immersion blender to purée the apple-pumpkin in the slow cooker.

5. Store in an airtight container in the refrigerator for up to 1 month.

Variation: Replace the pumpkin purée with 2 cups dried figs, stems removed, for an **Apple-Fig Butter.**

This butter is terrific for use on toast, pancakes, sandwiches, or even as a sweet glaze for meats.

Different varieties of apples produce slightly different results. Granny Smith or other tart varieties give a more acidic bite, while sweeter varieties like Red Delicious produce a more sugary butter. The choice is up to you.

If you're cooking ahead, you can freeze the butter in resealable plastic freezer bags and store for up to 6 to 9 months. Or can the butter using traditional pressure canning methods.

Replace that commercially prepared bottled ketchup with your own homemade version using this simple recipe. You'll be pleasantly surprise by the bold flavors that turn ketchup into a whole new experience.

Yield	2 cups
Serving Size	1 cup
Prep Time	10 minutes
Cook Time	8 hours

4 lb. (2kg) roma tomatoes, cored and diced

1 small yellow onion, diced

2/3 cup apple cider vinegar

1/4 cup brown sugar, firmly packed

2 tsp. salt

1/2 tsp. dry mustard powder

1/2 tsp. crushed red pepper flakes

1/4 tsp. ground cinnamon

1/4 tsp. ground allspice

1/4 tsp. ground nutmeg

1/4 tsp. ground ginger

1/8 tsp. ground cloves

1. In a 6- to 8-quart (5.5- to 7.5-liter) slow cooker, add roma tomatoes and yellow onion.

2. Pour in apple cider vinegar, and stir in brown sugar, salt, dry mustard powder, crushed red pepper flakes, cinnamon, allspice, nutmeg, ginger, and cloves.

3. Cover and cook on low for 8 hours.

4. Transfer ketchup to a blender or a food processor fitted with an S blade in batches, and purée.

5. Strain ketchup through a fine mesh strainer to remove the excess liquid.

6. Store in a plastic storage container or glass canning jar in the refrigerator for up to 1 month.

Variation: For an Asian version, replace the apple cider vinegar with rice wine vinegar and add 1 tablespoon soy sauce and 1/2 teaspoon sesame seeds.

For a smoother-textured ketchup, you can remove the tomato skins before you dice them. An easy way to peel tomatoes is to bring a large pot of water to a boil over high heat. Add tomatoes and blanch for 30 to 60 seconds. Use tongs to remove tomatoes and immediately plunge them into a large bowl filled with ice and water. You'll see the skins crack and start to peel. Then, just use your fingers to pull away the skin and peel the tomato.

Homemade Ketchup

Tomato-Bacon Chutney

This chutney packs a powerful punch of flavor, thanks to the smoky bacon; acidic tomatoes; and the woody, evergreen scent of rosemary. Your taste buds will love the complex flavors of this tasty treat.

Yield	4 cups
Serving Size	¼ cup
Prep Time	20 minutes
Cook Time	3½ to 4 hours

1½ lb. (680g) bacon, sliced and diced

2 large yellow onions, diced

5 cloves garlic, peeled and minced

½ cup apple cider vinegar

½ cup brown sugar, firmly packed

¼ cup honey

2 (15-oz.; 420g) cans diced tomatoes, drained

2 tsp. ground paprika

1 tsp. dried rosemary

¼ tsp. salt

¼ tsp. black pepper

1. In a large skillet over medium-high heat, cook bacon, flipping every 60 seconds, for 12 to 15 minutes or until crispy. Drain on a paper towel–covered plate.

2. In a 6- to 8-quart (5.5- to 7.5-liter) slow cooker, combine bacon, yellow onions, garlic, apple cider vinegar, brown sugar, honey, tomatoes, paprika, rosemary, salt, and black pepper.

3. Cover and cook on high for 3½ to 4 hours.

4. Serve as either a hot or cold condiment. Store in an airtight container in the refrigerator for up to 2 weeks.

Measuring honey can get a bit sticky. Spray your measuring cup with nonstick cooking spray before measuring the honey. This helps the honey pour right out.

Chapter 4

Warming Soups, Stews, and Chilies

Low and slow is the perfect way to cook soups, stews, and chilies. Instead of tending a pot over a hot stove for what can sometimes be hours, the slow cooker does the work for you, making it the perfect tool for creating complex flavors and tender meats in soups, stews, and chilies.

A hot bowl of tomato soup is the perfect comfort food on a cold or rainy day. Sweet, acidic tomatoes are classically paired with basil and garlic in this warm, satisfying soup

Yield	8 cups
Serving Size	1 cup
Prep Time	15 minutes
Cook Time	6 to 8 hours

4 lb. (2kg) roma tomatoes, cored and diced

1 medium yellow onion, diced

2 medium carrots, peeled and diced

2 medium celery ribs, sliced

4 cloves garlic, minced

1 tsp. dried basil

1½ tsp. salt

¼ tsp. black pepper

2 cups chicken broth

1 cup heavy cream

1. In a 6- to 8-quart (5.5- to 7.5-liter) slow cooker, place roma tomatoes, yellow onion, carrots, celery, garlic, basil, salt, and black pepper.

2. Pour in chicken broth.

3. Cover and cook on low for 6 to 8 hours.

4. Transfer soup, in batches, to a blender or a food processor fitted with an S blade, and purée for 1 or 2 minutes or until smooth.

5. Stir in heavy cream before serving.

Variation: Add 1 teaspoon crushed red pepper flakes for a spicy tomato soup.

Be careful when transferring soup to a blender or a food processor. Overfilling a blender especially can lead to soup explosions, so avoid filling it more than half full. Also watch for pressure buildup when you put on the lid. Slow cooker soups are not at boiling temperature, but the steam they emit could still build up pressure in the blender, creating a vacuum effect. Pressure buildup could lead to heat explosions, so be sure you ventilate or cool your soup before puréeing it. Place the top on loosely, and cover it with a kitchen towel to stay on the safe side. You also can use an immersion blender. This handheld stick blender enables you to purée soup right in the pot. No transferring required!

Tomato Bisque

Zuppa Toscana
(Tuscan Soup)

The time-honored pairing of sausage and potatoes creates a creamy broth complete with kale. Spicy, hot sausage gives the soup a kick of both heat and flavor.

Yield	12 cups
Serving Size	2 cups
Prep Time	10 minutes
Cook Time	6 to 8 hours

3 russet potatoes, peeled and cut into 1-in. (2.5cm) chunks

1 medium yellow onion, peeled and diced

4 cups chicken broth

3 cloves garlic, minced

1 tsp. salt

1 lb. (450g) hot sausage, in casings

4 cups chopped kale leaves, loosely packed

1 cup heavy cream

1. In a 6- to 8-quart (5.5- to 7.5-liter) slow cooker, place russet potatoes.

2. Add yellow onion, pour in chicken broth, and stir in garlic and salt. Place hot sausage on top of soup.

3. Cover and cook on low for 6 to 8 hours.

4. During the last hour of cooking, remove sausage from the slow cooker, slice it, and return it to the slow cooker.

5. Stir in kale and heavy cream.

6. Cover, and continue to cook 1 hour.

Variation: You can use ground sausage in place of whole sausage. Brown the ground sausage in a large skillet over medium-high heat for 5 to 7 minutes or until completely browned. Drain the excess fat, and add the sausage to the slow cooker with the potatoes and onion.

Kale is a tougher leafy green that holds up really well in soups and especially in slow cooking, whereas some other leafy greens like spinach wilt quickly. You add the kale during the last hour of cooking to give it time to soften a bit. If you want to be able to eat the soup right away, use fresh spinach leaves instead, which will wilt immediately upon being stirred into the soup.

You can add the heavy cream at the same time without any further cooking.

Broccoli is the star of this rich and creamy soup that's loaded with chunks of fresh broccoli and gooey cheddar cheese.

Yield	12 cups
Serving Size	2 cups
Prep Time	10 minutes
Cook Time	3 or 4 hours

2 medium (1-lb.; 450g) bunches broccoli, cut into florets (4 cups)

1 medium yellow onion, diced

4 cloves garlic, minced

4 cups half-and-half

2 cups milk

1½ tsp. salt

3 cups shredded cheddar cheese

1. In a 6- to 8-quart (5.5- to 7.5-liter) slow cooker, place broccoli, yellow onion, and garlic.

2. Pour in half-and-half and milk, and stir in salt.

3. Cover and cook on low for 3 or 4 hours.

4. Before serving, stir in cheddar cheese until melted.

Variation: Add cooked and crumbled bacon when ready to serve for a smoky flavor addition.

This soup has a much shorter cooking time than most soups in this chapter. The broccoli cooks rather quickly and will end up mushy if overcooked. This short cooking time allows for the use of milk and half-and-half, which can curdle if cooked at a too-high heat.

For a more developed flavor, sauté the onions in 1 tablespoon olive oil in a skillet over medium-high heat for 5 to 7 minutes before adding them into the slow cooker.

Creamy Broccoli Cheese Soup

Spiced Butternut Squash Soup

Classic fall flavors of cinnamon, nutmeg, and ginger get a blast of heat with crushed red pepper flakes in this creamy, sweet, and spicy soup.

Yield	8 cups
Serving Size	1 cup
Prep Time	10 minutes
Cook Time	6 to 8 hours

2½ lb. (1.25kg) butternut squash, peeled, seeded, and cubed

1 medium yellow onion, diced

1 tsp. salt

½ tsp. ground cinnamon

¼ tsp. ground nutmeg

¼ tsp. ground ginger

¼ tsp. crushed red pepper flakes

4 cups chicken broth

1 cup heavy cream

1. In a 6- to 8-quart (5.5- to 7.5-liter) slow cooker, place butternut squash, yellow onion, salt, cinnamon, nutmeg, ginger, and crushed red pepper flakes.

2. Pour in chicken broth, and stir to combine.

3. Cover and cook on low for 6 to 8 hours or until butternut squash is tender.

4. Transfer in batches to a blender or a food processor fitted with an S blade, and purée until smooth.

5. Stir in heavy cream before serving.

You can use this recipe as a base for other winter squashes quite easily. Simply replace the butternut squash with a similar-size pumpkin, acorn squash, or kabocha squash. Each variation of squash produces a slightly different flavor, but all work well with the spicing of the soup. The only common winter squash to avoid in this recipe is spaghetti squash. It's far too stringy to work well in a soup.

Tender, orange sweet potatoes are the highlight of this bright and flavorful vegetarian chili. Cinnamon complements the sweetness of the sweet potatoes while cayenne provides some heat for a perfect balance between sweet and savory.

Yield	12 cups
Serving Size	2 cups
Prep Time	15 minutes
Cook Time	6 to 8 hours

6 medium sweet potatoes, peeled and cubed

1 medium white onion, diced

3 medium celery stalks, sliced

2 large tomatoes, diced

2 cloves garlic, crushed

1 (15-oz.; 420g) can black beans, drained and rinsed

2 tsp. paprika

2 tsp. ground mustard

1 tsp. dried basil

1 tsp. salt

¼ tsp. ground cinnamon

¼ tsp. cayenne

2 cups vegetable broth

1½ TB. soy sauce

1 bay leaf

1. In a 6- to 8-quart (5.5- to 7.5-liter) slow cooker, place sweet potatoes, white onion, celery, tomatoes, garlic, and black beans.

2. Season with paprika, mustard, basil, salt, cinnamon, and cayenne.

3. Pour in vegetable broth and soy sauce, and stir to combine.

4. Tuck bay leaf down into liquid.

5. Cover and cook on low for 6 to 8 hours.

6. Remove bay leaf before serving.

The terms *sweet potato* and *yam* are often erroneously used synonymously in the United States. It can be quite confusing when you spot sweet potatoes and yams next to each other in the produce section with two visually different tubers. They're actually two different kinds of sweet potatoes. One has a golden skin and cream-colored flesh, and the other has a copper skin with bright orange flesh. The latter is often referred to as a *yam* to distinguish between the two varieties.

Actual yams have a dark, rough skin with red or purple flesh and are difficult to find in many grocery stores because they're native to Africa and Asia, and the demand for exportation is often low.

Vegetarian Sweet Potato Chili

Chicken Taco Soup

Loaded with beans, tomatoes, onions, and chiles, this soup contains everything a taco has to offer, all in a convenient, hearty, filling soup.

Yield	12 cups
Serving Size	2 cups
Prep Time	15 minutes
Cook Time	6 to 8 hours

2 lb. (1kg) boneless, skinless chicken breasts

1 medium yellow onion, diced

2 cloves garlic, crushed

1 cup frozen corn kernels, thawed

1 (15-oz.; 420g) can pinto beans, drained and rinsed

1 (15-oz.; 420g) can kidney beans, drained and rinsed

2 (15-oz.; 420g) cans diced tomatoes, with juice

2 (4-oz.; 110g) cans diced green chiles, with liquid

2 tsp. paprika

1½ tsp. salt

1 tsp. chili powder

1 tsp. dried oregano

1 tsp. ground cumin

½ tsp. crushed red pepper flakes

6 cups chicken broth

Juice of 1 medium lime

1. Trim chicken of all fat, and cut into 1-inch (2.5-centimeter) cubes. Transfer chicken to a 6- to 8-quart (5.5- to 7.5-liter) slow cooker.

2. Add yellow onion, garlic, corn, pinto beans, kidney beans, tomatoes, green chiles, paprika, salt, chili powder, oregano, cumin, and crushed red pepper flakes.

3. Pour in chicken broth and stir to combine.

4. Cover and cook on low for 6 to 8 hours.

5. Stir in lime juice before serving.

Variation: For **Beef Taco Soup,** substitute 2 pounds (1 kilogram) ground beef in place of the chicken. Brown the meat in a skillet over medium heat for 5 to 7 minutes, breaking up chunks with a spoon, and drain off any excess fat before adding the beef to the slow cooker in step 1.

Toppings aren't necessary with this soup, but a dollop of sour cream, shredded cheddar cheese, and chopped fresh green onions or cilantro provide an extra layer of flavor to this soup.

Before using canned beans in a recipe, drain and rinse them—unless you're otherwise directed in the recipe. Beans are canned in a thick, starchy liquid that can discolor your finished dish. The liquid also contains sodium, which may lead to an overly salty recipe.

This simple broth-based version of the classic comfort soup combines the mild sweetness of leeks with the soothing flavors of chicken broth and potatoes.

3 leeks, halved and sliced

8 medium red potatoes, diced

¼ cup butter

4 cups chicken broth

1 tsp. salt

1. In a 6- to 8-quart (5.5- to 7.5-liter) slow cooker, place leeks, red potatoes, and butter.

2. Pour in chicken broth, and stir in salt.

3. Cover and cook on low for 6 to 8 hours.

Variation: Before serving, add 1 cup heavy whipping cream for a creamy soup base. Serve chunky, or purée in a blender or a food processor fitted with an S blade for a smooth soup.

Leeks are a member of the onion family and have a mild but distinct flavor. The leek's white stem is the edible part.

Leeks easily hang on to the soil they're grown in, so be sure to clean them well before adding them to your recipe. Trim off the stringy roots and long green leaves, slice the leeks lengthwise, and rinse out any dirt or debris that might be inside any of the layers.

Winter Leek and Potato Soup

Russian Red Borscht

This hot beet soup is tangy and sour and packed with vegetables. Known for its bold, deep red color, this borscht is just as bold in its flavor. Caraway and dill provide a familiar yet exotic flavor combination.

Yield	12 cups
Serving Size	2 cups
Prep Time	15 minutes
Cook Time	6 to 8 hours

6 medium fresh beets, tops removed, peeled, and diced

2 medium russet potatoes, peeled and diced

1 medium yellow onion, diced

4 medium carrots, peeled and diced

1 (15-oz.; 420g) can kidney beans, drained and rinsed

5 cloves garlic, minced

1 TB. brown sugar, firmly packed

1½ tsp. salt

1 tsp. dried dill weed

½ tsp. caraway seeds

¼ tsp. black pepper

¼ cup apple cider vinegar

4 cups beef broth

1 bay leaf

4 cups shredded cabbage

Juice of 1 medium lemon

1. In a 6- to 8-quart (5.5- to 7.5-liter) slow cooker, place beets, russet potatoes, yellow onion, carrots, kidney beans, and garlic.

2. Sprinkle brown sugar, salt, dill weed, caraway seeds, and black pepper over vegetables.

3. Pour in apple cider vinegar and beef broth.

4. Tuck bay leaf down into liquid.

5. Cover and cook on low for 6 to 8 hours.

6. Add cabbage during the last hour of cooking.

7. Remove bay leaf and stir in lemon juice just before serving.

Variation: For a smooth borscht, transfer the soup in batches to a blender or a food processor fitted with an S blade to purée.

Borscht is a classic Eastern European soup known for its deep red color. It's often served topped with a dollop of sour cream and garnished with fresh dill or parsley.

This creamy chowder is refreshingly light yet filling. Sweet corn combines with mild potatoes and celery and sharp onion for a warm, comforting, creamy soup.

Yield	12 cups
Serving Size	2 cups
Prep Time	10 minutes
Cook Time	4½ to 6½ hours

4 cups frozen corn kernels, thawed

3 medium russet potatoes, peeled and cut into 1-in. (2.5cm) pieces

1 medium yellow onion, diced

5 medium stalks celery, sliced

2 TB. sugar

2 tsp. salt

2 cups chicken broth

3 cups half-and-half

1. In a 6- to 8-quart (5.5- to 7.5-liter) slow cooker, place corn, russet potatoes, yellow onion, and celery.

2. Sprinkle sugar and salt over vegetables.

3. Pour in chicken broth.

4. Cover and cook on low for 4 to 6 hours.

5. Pour in half-and-half, increase heat to high, and cook for 30 more minutes.

Variation: For a meaty **Chicken Corn Chowder,** add 2 pounds (1 kilogram) boneless, skinless chicken breast, trimmed and cut into 1-inch (2.5-centimeter) cubes at the same time as the corn, potatoes, onion, and celery.

You can use fresh, canned, or frozen corn in this recipe. If you opt for fresh, 1 ear of corn yields approximately ½ cup corn kernels. Simply shuck the corn and run a sharp knife between the kernels and the cob from one end to another to remove the kernels. If you opt for canned corn, use a 16-ounce (450-gram) can. Drain the liquid from the can before using the corn in a recipe.

Comfort Corn Chowder

Old-Fashioned Beef Stew

Tender chunks of beef slowly simmer with potatoes, carrots, and celery in this thick and hearty stew. Pearl onions and herbs add to the depth of flavor.

Yield	12 cups
Serving Size	2 cups
Prep Time	15 minutes
Cook Time	8 to 10 hours

2 TB. vegetable oil

2 lb. (1kg) beef stew meat, cubed

2 TB. cornstarch

8 medium red potatoes, cut into 1-in. (2.5cm) chunks

1 lb. (450g) pearl or boiling onions, peeled

4 medium carrots, peeled and sliced

4 medium stalks celery, sliced

2 cloves garlic, minced

1 tsp. salt

1 tsp. sugar

½ tsp. black pepper

½ tsp. dried rosemary

½ tsp. dried parsley

½ tsp. paprika

¼ tsp. dried oregano

¼ tsp. dried basil

¼ tsp. ground allspice

2 cups beef broth

2 TB. Worcestershire sauce

1 bay leaf

1. In a large skillet over medium-high heat, heat vegetable oil. Add beef stew meat, and sear for about 2 minutes per side.

2. Dust meat with cornstarch, and cook for 1 minute to sear cornstarch to meat. Transfer meat to a 6- to 8-quart (5.5- to 7.5-liter) slow cooker.

3. Add red potatoes, pearl onions, carrots, celery, and garlic to the slow cooker, and season with salt, sugar, black pepper, rosemary, parsley, paprika, oregano, basil, and allspice.

4. Pour in beef broth and Worcestershire sauce, and stir briefly to combine.

5. Tuck bay leaf down into liquid.

6. Cover and cook on low for 8 to 10 hours.

7. Remove bay leaf before serving.

Variation: If you can't find pearl onions, you can use 1 medium yellow or white onion, peeled and diced.

Cornstarch is often used as a thickening agent in soups and stews. But you can't just dump the cornstarch into a liquid, or you'll end up with clumps of cornstarch floating around in your soup. Instead, the cornstarch or other thickening agent needs to bond with some sort of fat. In this recipe, the cornstarch bonds with both the meat and the olive oil. This allows it to spread evenly throughout the soup and thicken the liquid as it cooks. Flour is another common thickening agent.

In this rich and hearty stew, tender, slow-simmered pork combines with the Mexican flavor influences of cumin, garlic, and green chile. Cayenne offers a spicy kick.

Yield	12 cups
Serving Size	2 cups
Prep Time	15 minutes
Cook Time	8 to 10 hours

2 medium russet potatoes, peeled and cut into 1-in. (2.5cm) cubes

3 medium carrots, peeled and diced

1 medium yellow onion, diced

1 large tomato, diced

3 cloves garlic, crushed

2 lb. (1kg) boneless pork loin roast, trimmed, and cut into 1-in. (2.5cm) cubes

1½ tsp. salt

1 tsp. dried oregano

1 tsp. ground cumin

½ tsp. black pepper

½ tsp. cayenne

1 bay leaf

4 cups chicken broth

1 (10-oz.; 285g) can whole green chiles, drained and roughly chopped

1. In a 6- to 8-quart (5.5- to 7.5-liter) slow cooker, layer russet potatoes, carrots, and yellow onion. Top with tomato and garlic.

2. Place pork loin roast on top of vegetables.

3. Season with salt, oregano, cumin, black pepper, and cayenne, and add bay leaf.

4. Pour chicken broth over meat and vegetables.

5. Cover and cook on low for 6 to 8 hours.

6. Remove bay leaf and stir in green chiles before serving.

The canned green chiles are added at the end of this recipe so they maintain their flavor. Because canned green chiles are already cooked in the canning process, additional long, slow cooking dilutes the flavor. This stew highlights the green chiles, so you want to add them at the end so they provide the most flavor.

Green Chile Pork Stew

Texas-Style Beef Chili

Texas would be proud of this no-bean chili in which meaty, tender beef is the star. Perfectly spiced, with a balance of heat and flavor, this chili is a hearty, filling, cowboy-style meal.

Yield	12 cups
Serving Size	2 cups
Prep Time	15 minutes
Cook Time	8 hours

2 lb. (1kg) beef chuck roast, trimmed of fat and cut into ½-in. (2.5cm) cubes

1 medium yellow onion, diced

2 large red bell peppers, ribs and seeds removed, and diced

2 medium stalks celery, sliced

1 (15-oz.; 420g) can diced tomatoes, with juice

1 (4-oz.; 110g) can diced green chiles, with liquid

2 TB. tomato paste

1 TB. chili powder

2 tsp. cumin

2 tsp. paprika

1 tsp. onion powder

1 tsp. garlic powder

1 tsp. salt

1 cup beef broth

2 TB. Worcestershire sauce

Juice of 1 medium lime

1. In a large skillet over high heat, sear beef chuck roast cubes on all 4 sides for about 60 seconds per side. Transfer beef to a 6- to 8-quart (5.5- to 7.5-liter) slow cooker.

2. Add yellow onion, red bell peppers, celery, diced tomatoes with juice, green chiles with liquid, and tomato paste to the slow cooker.

3. Season with chili powder, cumin, paprika, onion powder, garlic powder, and salt, and stir to combine.

4. Pour in beef broth and Worcestershire sauce.

5. Cover and cook on low for 8 to 10 hours.

6. Stir in lime juice before serving.

This chili tastes amazing just the way it is, but you also can add toppings for even more flavor. Shredded cheddar cheese, sour cream, and chopped fresh cilantro are ideal atop this Texas-style chili.

Tangy pineapple and sweet apple juice combine with savory flavors and spice in this beautifully balanced sweet pork chili.

Yield	12 cups
Serving Size	2 cups
Prep Time	15 minutes
Cook Time	8 to 10 hours

2 lb. (1kg) pork roast, trimmed, and cut into 1-in. (2.5cm) cubes

1 medium yellow bell pepper, stem ribs and seeds removed, and diced

3 cups cubed fresh pineapple

1 (15-oz.; 420g) can black beans, drained and rinsed

2 cups frozen corn kernels, thawed

1 (6-oz.; 170g) can tomato paste

3 medium tomatoes, diced

1 bunch green onions, sliced (1 cup)

4 cloves garlic, minced

3 TB. brown sugar

1 TB. paprika

2 tsp. salt

½ tsp. black pepper

½ tsp. chili powder

¼ tsp. ground cinnamon

1¼ cups apple juice

1 TB. apple cider vinegar

1. In a 6- to 8-quart (5.5- to 7.5-liter) slow cooker, place pork roast, yellow bell pepper, pineapple, black beans, corn, tomato paste, tomatoes, green onions, and garlic.

2. Sprinkle brown sugar, paprika, salt, black pepper, chili powder, and cinnamon in the slow cooker, and stir to combine.

3. Pour in apple juice and apple cider vinegar.

4. Cover and cook on low for 8 to 10 hours.

An average-size pineapple yields about 3 cups cubes. To cut a fresh pineapple, lay it on its side and slice off the top green leaves and the bottom end. Stand the pineapple upright, and carefully slice off the outer skin. Remove any eyes that remain, too.

Most commercially sold pineapples have a core that's pithy and tough. Freshly picked pineapple might not have this core. Use your finger or a butter knife to feel where the soft flesh turns tough on the top end of the pineapple. Run a butter knife around this to mark the core. Then use a sharp knife to slice off the soft flesh, leaving the core behind to discard.

Slow Braised Sweet Pork Chili

Indian-Style Spiced Chili

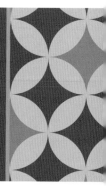

The spicy flavors of India meet American chili in this unusual and delightful twist on standard chili. Garam masala and cinnamon yield an exotic flavor while heavy cream adds an unusual creamy element your taste buds will love.

Yield	12 cups
Serving Size	2 cups
Prep Time	10 minutes
Cook Time	6 to 8 hours

2 lb. (1kg) boneless, skinless chicken breasts, cut into 1-in. (2.5cm) cubes

1 (15-oz.; 420g) can chickpeas, drained and rinsed

1 (15-oz.; 420g) can kidney beans, drained and rinsed

1 medium yellow onion, diced

1 jalapeño, stem removed, and minced

2 tsp. paprika

2 tsp. garam masala

1 tsp. ground cumin

½ tsp. ground cinnamon

½ tsp. salt

⅛ tsp. turmeric powder

1 (8-oz.; 225g) can tomato sauce

1 cup chicken broth

1 cup whipping cream

1. In a 6- to 8-quart (5.5- to 7.5-liter) slow cooker, place chicken, chickpeas, kidney beans, yellow onion, and jalapeño.

2. Stir in paprika, garam masala, cumin, cinnamon, salt, and turmeric powder.

3. Pour in tomato sauce and chicken broth.

4. Cover and cook on low for 6 to 8 hours.

5. Stir in whipping cream just before serving.

Garam masala is an Indian spice blend of cumin, coriander, cardamom, black pepper, cinnamon, cloves, and nutmeg. The whole spices are toasted and ground into a distinctly flavorful mixture. You can find garam masala in the spice section of most grocery stores.

In this rich, white, creamy chili, chicken, white cannellini beans, and green chiles are slowly simmered, thickened with cream cheese, and splashed with heavy cream before serving. Lime juice adds a zip of acidity.

Yield	12 cups
Serving Size	2 cups
Prep Time	30 minutes
Cook Time	8 hours

2 lb. (1kg) chicken breast, trimmed and cut into 1-in. (2.5cm) cubes

2 (15-oz.; 420g) cans cannellini beans, drained and rinsed

2 (4-oz.; 110g) cans diced green chiles, with liquid

1 medium yellow onion, diced

1 jalapeño, stem removed, and minced

4 cloves garlic, minced

1 TB. ground cumin

1½ tsp. salt

1½ tsp. ground coriander

1 tsp. chili powder

4 cups chicken broth

1 cup heavy whipping cream

8 oz. (225g) cream cheese, cubed

Juice of 2 medium limes

1. In a 6- to 8-quart (5.5- to 7.5-liter) slow cooker, place chicken, cannellini beans, green chiles with liquid, yellow onion, jalapeño, and garlic.

2. Season with cumin, salt, coriander, and chili powder, and stir to combine.

3. Pour in chicken broth.

4. Cover and cook on low for 6 to 8 hours.

5. When just about ready to serve, stir in heavy whipping cream and cream cheese until cream cheese melts.

6. Stir in lime juice immediately before serving.

Successfully melting cream cheese into a soup or chili requires two elements: the cheese needs to be cut into cubes, and the soup needs to be stirred continuously until the cheese is completely melted. Simply letting the chili sit and then try to stir the cream cheese until it's smooth doesn't work and results in a lumpy chili. Small pieces and constant movement enable the soft cheese to more easily incorporate with the other liquids.

White Chicken Chili

Chapter 5

Super Sandwiches

If you like shredded meat sandwiches, the slow cooker is the perfect tool for you. It's a hassle-free way to make tender, meaty sandwiches. Even better, it's a great helper when you want to serve hot sandwiches to a crowd.

One note before we begin: meat weights vary, and the amounts listed in the recipes in this chapter are simply a suggested size range. When purchasing meat, look for a product nearest to the weight range suggested in the recipe.

Balsamic Beef Dip Sandwiches

Hot shredded beef roast simmered in a sweet and tangy *au jus* and served on a French roll makes the perfect dipping sandwich.

Yield	6 sandwiches
Serving Size	1 sandwich
Prep Time	5 minutes
Cook Time	8 to 10 hours

1 (3- or 4-lb.; 1.5- to 2kg) boneless beef chuck or round roast

1 cup beef broth

½ cup balsamic vinegar

2 TB. Worcestershire sauce

1 TB. honey

1 tsp. salt

½ tsp. garlic powder

½ tsp. onion powder

6 French sandwich rolls, sliced

1. Slice beef chuck roast into ½-inch-thick (1.25-centimeters-thick) strips, and place in a 6- to 8-quart (5.5- to 7.5-liter) slow cooker.

2. In a medium bowl, whisk together beef broth, balsamic vinegar, Worcestershire sauce, honey, salt, garlic powder, and onion powder. Pour over roast in the slow cooker.

3. Cover and cook on low for 8 to 10 hours.

4. Using a fork, shred meat in the slow cooker. Strain meat from juices, reserving juices to use as an au jus.

5. Serve hot on French rolls with au jus on the side for dipping.

Variation: Peel, halve, and slice 1 medium red onion, and place onion on top of the roast after step 1. Serve hot on French rolls topped with sliced pepperoncinis.

Au jus is a French term meaning "with juice." The *jus* in this recipe comes from the natural juices of the meat and is enhanced by the added flavorings. You can serve the sandwich without the *au jus,* but the dipping *jus* really enhances the flavor.

Thin-sliced steak, smothered with seasoned bell peppers, onions, and provolone cheese, make this sandwich as mouthwatering as it is messy.

Yield	6 sandwiches
Serving Size	1 sandwich
Prep Time	5 minutes
Cook Time	6 to 8 hours

2 lb. (1kg) round steak, ½-in. (1.25cm) slices

4 large green, red, yellow, or orange bell peppers, stems ribs and seeds removed, and sliced

1 medium red onion, halved and sliced

2 tsp. sugar

1 tsp. salt

1 tsp. garlic powder

½ tsp. dried oregano

½ tsp. dried basil

½ tsp. black pepper

6 hoagie rolls, sliced

6 slices provolone cheese

1. In a 6- to 8-quart (5.5- to 7.5-liter) slow cooker, place round steak, green bell peppers, and red onion.

2. Season meat and vegetables with sugar, salt, garlic powder, oregano, basil, and black pepper, and stir to combine.

3. Cover and cook on low for 6 to 8 hours.

4. Preheat the broiler.

5. Strain any excess liquids from the slow cooker, and spoon about 1 cup meat mixture onto each hoagie roll.

6. Top each sandwich with 1 slice provolone cheese.

7. Place sandwiches on a baking sheet and broil for 2 or 3 minutes, or until cheese is melted and bubbly.

8. Serve hot.

Variation: Add 1 pound (450 grams) button mushrooms (or your favorite), sliced, when you add the bell peppers and onion in step 1.

Toasting bread to use for hot sandwiches helps keep it from getting overly soggy with the hot meat and accompanying liquids. Simply toast in a toaster or under a broiler until browned, and you'll love the results.

Philly Cheesesteak Sandwiches

Extra-Sloppy Joes

Sloppy joes get a slow cooker makeover in this recipe. The low, slow cooking deepens the flavors, giving you a sandwich bursting with flavor. One warning: these can get messy, so napkins are required!

Yield	8 sandwiches
Serving Size	1 sandwich
Prep Time	10 minutes
Cook Time	4 to 6 hours

1 lb. (450g) lean ground beef

1 medium yellow onion, halved and sliced

1 large green bell pepper, ribs and seeds removed, and diced

2 medium stalks celery, diced

2 medium carrots, peeled and diced

1 (8-oz.; 225g) can tomato sauce

1 (6-oz.; 170g) can tomato paste

2 TB. Worcestershire sauce

4 cloves garlic, peeled and minced

1 TB. brown sugar, firmly packed

1 tsp. salt

1 tsp. ground mustard

½ tsp. crushed red pepper flakes

8 hamburger buns

1. In a large skillet over medium-high heat, cook ground beef and yellow onion, stirring occasionally, for about 5 minutes or until beef is browned.

2. Drain any excess fat from the skillet, and transfer beef and onions to a 6- to 8-quart (5.5- to 7.5-liter) slow cooker.

3. Add green bell pepper, celery, carrots, tomato sauce, tomato paste, Worcestershire sauce, garlic, brown sugar, salt, mustard, and crushed red pepper flakes, and stir to combine.

4. Cover and cook on low for 4 to 6 hours.

5. Spoon about ½ to ¾ cup meat on each hamburger bun and serve hot.

Variation: For a lighter version, use 1 pound (450 grams) ground turkey in place of the ground beef.

Before adding ground meats to a slow cooker, first brown it in a skillet on the stove to remove the excess fat. (There are a few exceptions to this rule, as explained elsewhere in the book.) When browning the meat, you don't have to completely cook it because it will cook thoroughly in the slow cooker. You simply need to brown it to the point that the excess fats are released so you can drain them off.

Spicy chicken is covered with melting cheese and heaps of slow roasted red peppers in this delicious Italian sandwich served on focaccia.

Yield	6 sandwiches
Serving Size	1 sandwich
Prep Time	5 minutes
Cook Time	4 to 6 hours

2 lb. (1kg) boneless, skinless chicken breasts, trimmed

2 TB. olive oil

½ tsp. salt

½ tsp. garlic powder

½ tsp. dried basil

¼ tsp. dried oregano

¼ tsp. crushed red pepper flakes

⅛ tsp. black pepper

2 large red bell peppers, ribs and seeds removed, and sliced

2 cups shredded mozzarella cheese

2 (1-lb.; 450g) loaves focaccia

2 cups fresh spinach leaves

1. In a 6- to 8-quart (5.5- to 7.5-liter) slow cooker, place chicken breasts.

2. Drizzle olive oil over chicken, and season with salt, garlic powder, basil, oregano, crushed red pepper flakes, and black pepper.

3. Arrange red bell pepper slices over chicken.

4. Cover and cook on low for 4 to 6 hours.

5. Using a fork, pull apart chicken into large chunks, or cut into slices using a knife. Top immediately with mozzarella cheese, and allow cheese to melt.

6. Cut each focaccia loaf into 3 pieces. To create 6 sandwiches, split each piece horizontally to create sandwich tops and bottoms.

7. Spoon ½ cup chicken, peppers, and cheese on each sandwich. Top with ⅓ cup spinach leaves and serve.

Variation: These sandwiches are great served with a quick and easy garlic aioli. In a small bowl, combine ½ cup mayonnaise with 3 cloves crushed garlic, 1 tablespoon lemon juice, and ½ teaspoon salt.

It's a common misconception that you have to cook meats in the slow cooker with a lot of liquid. Some meats require the slow braising and simmering, but others just need the low, slow heat a slow cooker provides. In this recipe, the chicken breast is cooked without any braising or simmering. Instead, olive oil is used to keep the meat from drying out. This also keeps the chicken from completely falling apart and shredding as it cooks.

Spicy Italian Chicken Sandwiches

Greek Chicken Gyros

Zippy chicken breast topped with lemon juice and garlic is served in a pita flatbread with tangy cucumber yogurt tzatziki sauce in this slow cooked version of the classic Greek gyro sandwich.

Yield	6 sandwiches
Serving Size	1 sandwich
Prep Time	10 minutes
Cook Time	4 to 6 hours

1 medium red onion, halved and thinly sliced

2 lb. (1kg) boneless, skinless chicken breasts, trimmed

¼ cup red wine vinegar

Juice of 1 medium lemon

1 TB. olive oil

6 cloves garlic, minced

½ tsp. dried oregano

½ tsp. dried basil

⅛ tsp. black pepper

Zest of 1 medium lemon

1 cup plain Greek yogurt

2 TB. fresh dill, minced

¼ tsp. salt

1 medium cucumber, peeled

6 pita or Arabic flatbreads

3 cups romaine lettuce, chopped

2 roma tomatoes, sliced

1. In the bottom a 6- to 8-quart (5.5- to 7.5-liter) slow cooker, layer half of red onions, reserving remaining half for use as a topping. Place chicken breasts on top of onions.

2. Pour red wine vinegar and lemon juice over chicken, and drizzle with olive oil.

3. Sprinkle 6 cloves minced garlic over chicken breasts, followed by oregano, basil, black pepper, and lemon zest.

4. Cover and cook on low for 4 to 6 hours.

5. In a medium bowl, combine Greek yogurt, dill, and salt.

6. Cut cucumber in half. Finely dice half of cucumber, and thinly slice remaining half. Stir diced cucumbers into yogurt mixture, and refrigerate until ready to serve. Set aside sliced cucumbers.

7. To serve, spoon ½ cup chicken on half of each pita, and top with ½ cup romaine lettuce, a few red onion slices, 4 to 6 slices cucumber, 3 to 5 roma tomato slices, and 1 heaping spoonful yogurt sauce. Fold over pita, and serve.

Variation: You can use other sauces and even salad dressings in place of the tzatziki sauce for a wide variety of sandwich flavors. Try ranch, honey mustard, Italian, or even blue cheese.

The yogurt sauce in this recipe is called *tzatziki sauce*. Of Greek and Turkish origin, it is most commonly served cold on grilled meats. The two serving methods are combined in the gyro (pronounced *YEE-ros*) sandwich. Lemon juice is sometimes included in the sauce for additional acidity.

In this mouthwatering sandwich, pork roast is simmered in a homemade barbecue mixture to produce a tender, pull-apart meat that's infused with the dark, sweet flavors of barbecue sauce.

Yield	8 sandwiches
Serving Size	1 sandwich
Prep Time	5 minutes
Cook Time	8 to 10 hours

1 (3- or 4-lb.; 1.5- to 2kg) boneless pork butt or shoulder roast

1 medium yellow onion, halved and sliced

1 cup ketchup

¼ cup brown sugar, firmly packed

¼ cup Worcestershire sauce

2 TB. red wine vinegar

2 tsp. garlic powder

½ tsp. salt

½ tsp. crushed red pepper flakes

½ tsp. ground mustard

8 hamburger buns

1. Slice pork butt roast into ½-inch-thick (1.25-centimeters-thick) pieces, and place in a 6- to 8-quart (5.5- to 7.5-liter) slow cooker. Top with yellow onion slices.

2. In a small bowl, combine ketchup, brown sugar, Worcestershire sauce, red wine vinegar, garlic powder, salt, crushed red pepper flakes, and mustard. Pour sauce over pork.

3. Cover and cook on low for 8 to 10 hours.

4. Using a fork, shred meat.

5. Spoon ¾ to 1 cup meat on each hamburger bun, and serve hot.

Variation: Add 2 teaspoons liquid smoke for a nice, smoky flavor.

If you want to use bottled barbecue sauce instead of making your own, you need to change the recipe slightly to avoid burning the barbecue sauce. Proceed with step 1 as directed. Then, instead of following step 2, add 2 cups water to the slow cooker. Cover and cook on low for 8 to 10 hours, and drain excess liquid from the slow cooker. Shred pork as directed in step 4, and add 2 cups bottled barbecue sauce. Serve immediately, or let heat through on low for 1 hour.

Barbecue Pulled Pork Sandwiches

Vietnamese Pulled Pork Banh Mi

Tender Vietnamese shredded pork with pickled vegetables, hot jalapeño slices, and fresh cilantro served on a crusty French baguette makes for a sensational variation of this trendy Vietnamese sandwich.

Yield	6 sandwiches
Serving Size	1 sandwich
Prep Time	10 minutes
Cook Time	8 to 10 hours

2 or 3 lb. (1 or 1.5kg) boneless pork butt or shoulder roast

1 cup chicken broth

¼ cup soy sauce

2 TB. fish sauce

½ tsp. ground ginger

3 cloves garlic, peeled and minced

1 medium daikon radish, julienned or shredded

2 large carrots, julienned or shredded

¼ cup rice vinegar

Juice of 1 medium lime

6 crusty baguettes, sliced

1 medium cucumber, sliced

3 cups fresh cilantro leaves

1 jalapeño, thinly sliced

1. In a 6- to 8-quart (5.5- to 7.5-liter) slow cooker, place pork butt roast.

2. Pour in chicken broth, soy sauce, and fish sauce, and stir in ginger and garlic.

3. Cover and cook on low for 8 to 10 hours.

4. Meanwhile, in a small bowl, combine daikon radish and carrots. Top with rice vinegar, cover, and refrigerate until ready to serve.

5. When just about ready to serve, shred pork and stir in lime juice.

6. Spoon ½ cup meat, hot or cold, onto each crusty baguette. Top with daikon radish and carrot mixture, cucumber slices, cilantro leaves, and jalapeño slices, and serve.

Fish sauce can be an intimidating ingredient if you've never worked with it before. It's one of those unusual ingredients that smells terrible but adds a real depth of flavor to a dish. You can omit the fish sauce in this recipe if you like, but the flavor of the meat might fall slightly flat as a result. The fish sauce develops those rich and tangy flavors of southeast Asia.

Chapter 6

Beef and Lamb Entrées

The slow cooker becomes the ideal braising tool for tough cuts of red meat that require long, slow cooking methods in order to create melt-in-your-mouth finished meals. In this chapter, we explore several takes on American beef and lamb classics, as well as some flavorful red meat recipes with world flair.

Due to the nature of red meat, the recipes in this chapter utilizing tougher cuts should be cooked on the low setting because they need a long, slow, and low cooking process to tenderize.

Flavorful, spicy beef melts in your mouth in this slow cooked Korean classic. Sweet and spicy, this barbecue-style beef dish is sure to please.

Yield	**2 pounds** (1 kilogram)
Serving Size	**⅓ pound** (150 grams)
Prep Time	**5 minutes**
Cook Time	**6 to 8 hours**

2 lb. (1kg) flank steak

⅓ cup soy sauce

¼ cup brown sugar, firmly packed

2 TB. sesame seeds

1 TB. sesame oil

3 cloves garlic, peeled and minced

½ tsp. crushed red pepper flakes

½ tsp. ground ginger

2 tsp. oyster sauce

½ cup sliced green onions, green parts only

1. Cut flank steak against the grain into ¼-inch-thick (10-centimeter-thick) strips. Place strips in a 6- to 8-quart (5.5- to 7.5-liter) slow cooker slow cooker.

2. In a small bowl, combine soy sauce, brown sugar, sesame seeds, sesame oil, garlic, crushed red pepper flakes, ginger, and oyster sauce. Pour over steak strips in the slow cooker.

3. Cover and cook on low for 6 to 8 hours.

4. Garnish with green onions and serve hot, alone, or over rice.

Cutting against the grain is important to remember when working with beef. Flank steak has a highly visible grain and looks almost striped. Think of the grain as the natural breaking point of the meat. Cutting against the grain ensures the maximum number of breaking points in each bite, ensuring every bite almost falls apart or melts in your mouth.

Korean Beef Bulgogi

Modern Meatloaf

This modern twist on the classic ground beef loaf has a nice level of heat for a full-flavored meatloaf, complete with a spicy glaze.

Yield	8 slices
Serving Size	1 slice
Prep Time	10 minutes
Cook Time	4 or 5 hours

1 lb. (450g) lean ground beef

½ medium yellow onion, diced

1 cup breadcrumbs

½ cup milk

3 TB. Worcestershire sauce

1 tsp. salt

1 tsp. dried basil

1 tsp. dried oregano

½ tsp. black pepper

½ tsp. crushed red pepper flakes

½ cup ketchup

2 TB. brown sugar

2 tsp. hot sauce

1. In a large bowl, combine ground beef, yellow onion, breadcrumbs, milk, 2 tablespoons Worcestershire sauce, salt, basil, oregano, black pepper, and crushed red pepper flakes.

2. Using your hands, knead meat mixture for about 1 minute or until well combined. Form meat into a loaf shape and place in a 6- to 8-quart (5.5- to 7.5-liter) slow cooker.

3. In a small bowl, combine ketchup, brown sugar, remaining 1 tablespoon Worcestershire sauce, and hot sauce. Pour sauce over loaf in the slow cooker.

4. Cover and cook on high 4 or 5 hours.

5. Slice and serve hot.

Variation: Ground flaxseed, wheat germ, and wheat bran are increasingly available health foods that are perfect substitutions for breadcrumbs. For a nutrient boost, use any combination of the three to replace the 1 cup breadcrumbs in this recipe.

Using a lean ground beef is important for a slow cooked meatloaf because in the slow cooker, the fat in the beef has nowhere to drain. Ground sirloin works particularly well because it has a low 8 to 10 percent fat content.

Seasoned chuck roast is slowly simmered for 8 hours surrounded by carrots and onions for a fall-apart-tender beef dish, perfect for a Sunday afternoon family dinner.

Yield	2 pounds (1 kilogram)
Serving Size	¼ pound (110 grams)
Prep Time	10 minutes
Cook Time	8 hours

1 (2- or 3-lb.; 1- to 1.5kg) chuck roast

½ tsp. salt

¼ tsp. black pepper

1 medium yellow onion, cut into large chunks

1 lb. (450g) carrots, peeled and cut into 2-in. (5cm) pieces

1 cup beef broth

2 TB. Worcestershire sauce

3 cloves garlic, minced

1. In a 6- to 8-quart (5.5- to 7.5-liter) slow cooker, place chuck roast.

2. Season with salt and black pepper.

3. Place yellow onion on top of roast, and surround roast with carrots.

4. Pour beef broth and Worcestershire sauce over carrots, and sprinkle garlic over roast and vegetables.

5. Cover and cook on low for 6 to 8 hours.

Variation: For a hearty one-pot meal, include additional vegetables such as 6 medium red potatoes, cut into bite-size chunks, and 4 medium stalks celery, sliced. Place the vegetables on the bottom of the slow cooker and the meat on top.

Pot roasts utilize large, tough cuts of beef, particularly the chuck. The fibrous meat slowly breaks down as it braises in the slow cooker, turning that tough, chewy meat into a tender and flavorful bite. Slow cooking on high is not recommended for this cut.

Sunday Afternoon Pot Roast

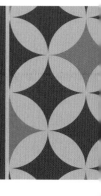

Braised Beef Short Ribs

Slow-braised beef short ribs fall right off the bone for a tender, succulent beef dish that warms you from the inside out.

Yield   **8 ribs**

Serving Size   **1 rib**

Prep Time   **5 minutes**

Cook Time   **8 hours**

1 TB. olive oil

8 beef short ribs

2 cups beef broth

¼ cup Worcestershire sauce

1 tsp. onion powder

1 tsp. garlic powder

1 tsp. salt

½ tsp. black pepper

1. In a large skillet over high heat, heat olive oil. Add short ribs and sear for about 30 seconds per side or until all exposed meat is browned. Remove from heat.

2. In a 6- to 8-quart (5.5- to 7.5-liter) slow cooker, combine beef broth, Worcestershire sauce, onion powder, and garlic powder.

3. Season short ribs with salt and black pepper, and place short ribs in the slow cooker braising liquids.

4. Cover and cook on low for 8 hours.

5. Serve hot.

Variation: These short ribs are terrific served over polenta. For an extra layer of flavor, replace 1 cup beef broth with 1 cup red wine.

Braising is typically reserved for tough cuts of meat. Traditional braising involves searing meat at a high heat and then finishing in a pot with a liquid. Slow cookers are a perfect braising tool because they can braise with a very low heat, allowing the tough collagen and fibers in the meat to slowly melt away.

You can buy short ribs boneless or bone-in. Both can be used in this recipe with the same cooking time.

Hearty beef ribs are made easy in this slow roasted version, complete with a homemade, hickory-smoked honey garlic barbecue sauce.

Yield	8 ribs
Serving Size	1 rib
Prep Time	5 minutes
Cook Time	8 hours

8 whole beef ribs

2 cups ketchup

12 cloves garlic, minced

2 TB. hot sauce

¼ cup honey

2 TB. molasses

2 TB. brown sugar

1 TB. hickory flavor liquid smoke

1 TB. cornstarch

1 tsp. Worcestershire sauce

1 tsp. soy sauce

1 tsp. salt

1 tsp. onion powder

1 tsp. garlic powder

1 tsp. dried oregano

1 tsp. dried basil

½ tsp. black pepper

¼ tsp. cayenne

¼ tsp. paprika

1. In a 6- to 8-quart (5.5- to 7.5-liter) slow cooker, place beef ribs. Cut ribs to fit and stack, if necessary.

2. In a medium bowl, combine ketchup, garlic, hot sauce, honey, molasses, brown sugar, liquid smoke, cornstarch, Worcestershire sauce, soy sauce, salt, onion powder, garlic powder, oregano, basil, black pepper, cayenne, and paprika.

3. Pour sauce over ribs in the slow cooker, being sure all ribs are coated with sauce.

4. Cover and cook on low for 8 to 10 hours.

5. Serve hot.

Ribs have a tough membrane on the bottom or back side that can create a chewy bite. You can remove it easily before cooking. Turn the ribs face down, and rub your fingers along the edge of a rib to release the membrane. It will easily loosen, and you can pull the plastic-like strip off the ribs.

Cooking on high is not recommended for this cut.

Honey Garlic Barbecue Beef Ribs

Midwestern Beef Brisket

Smoky brisket rubbed with flavorful spices makes for a hearty meal you'd never guess came from a humble slow cooker.

Yield	**3 pounds** (1.5 kilograms)
Serving Size	**⅓ pound** (150 grams)
Prep Time	**5 minutes**
Cook Time	**6 to 8 hours**

1 (3- or 4-lb.; 1.5- to 2kg) beef brisket

4 TB. liquid smoke

¼ cup Worcestershire sauce

1 tsp. salt

1 tsp. garlic powder

½ tsp. chili powder

½ tsp. paprika

½ tsp. onion powder

½ tsp. black pepper

½ tsp. cayenne

1 medium yellow onion, diced

1. In a 6- to 8-quart (5.5- to 7.5-liter) slow cooker, place beef brisket.

2. Pour liquid smoke and Worcestershire sauce over brisket.

3. In a small bowl, combine salt, garlic powder, chili powder, paprika, onion powder, black pepper, and cayenne. Rub spice mixture over top of brisket.

4. Top with yellow onion.

5. Cover and cook on low for 6 to 8 hours.

6. Serve hot.

Variation: You can adjust the spice rub used on the meat to your liking. For a **Jewish-Style Brisket,** use 1 cup red wine in place of the liquid smoke, and instead of the seasoning mixture called for in step 3, rub the brisket with a combination of 1 teaspoon salt, 1 teaspoon garlic powder, 1 teaspoon dried rosemary, 1 teaspoon dried oregano, ½ teaspoon black pepper, and ½ teaspoon dried basil.

The brisket is perhaps one of the toughest cuts of beef because it comes from the cow's pectoral muscles, which support the majority of the cow's weight. The tough connective tissue needs long, slow cooking in order to yield a tender result. Cooking on high is not recommended for this cut.

In traditional American cooking, brisket is often barbecued long and slow, or smoked. Jewish cooking calls for a braised method. Both styles can easily be replicated in the slow cooker.

Tender, slow roasted leg of lamb is classically paired with the flavors of rosemary, lemon, and garlic for this simple, slow cooked version of a traditionally elegant meal.

Yield	3 or 4 pounds (1.5 to 2 kilograms)
Serving Size	1/3 pound (150 grams)
Prep Time	5 minutes
Cook Time	8 to 10 hours

1 (4- to 6-lb.; 2- to 2.75kg) bone-in leg of lamb

Juice of 2 medium lemons

10 cloves garlic, minced

1 TB. dried rosemary

2 tsp. salt

1 tsp. black pepper

1 large yellow onion, diced

1. In a 6- to 8-quart (5.5- to 7.5-liter) slow cooker, place leg of lamb.

2. Pour lemon juice over lamb.

3. Rub lamb with garlic, rosemary, salt, and black pepper.

4. Sprinkle yellow onion over lamb.

5. Cover and cook on low for 8 to 10 hours.

6. Serve hot.

Variation: For extra flavor, pour 1/2 cup red wine over lamb along with lemon juice.

Leg of lamb is served both bone-in and in a boneless version. Either variety works well in this slow cooker recipe because we're not aiming for a rare or medium-rare doneness level, but rather a very tender meat.

Boneless leg of lamb is often sold with a netting around it to help hold its shape while cooking. You can leave on this netting because it's designed to withstand the heat. However, do remove it before serving.

Cooking on high is not recommended for this cut.

Leg of Lamb with Rosemary, Lemon, and Garlic

Triple Citrus Lamb Shanks

Tender lamb shank is slowly braised in the tangy citrus juices of orange, lemon, and lime. The vegetable-based braising liquid is tart and flavorful and provides a saucy addition to the succulent lamb.

Yield	6 shanks
Serving Size	1 shank
Prep Time	15 minutes
Cook Time	8 hours

2 TB. olive oil

6 whole lamb shanks

2 medium carrots, peeled and finely diced

2 medium celery stalks, finely diced

1 large sweet onion, minced

3 cloves garlic, minced

2 TB. tomato paste

1 cup chicken broth

1 tsp. salt

Zest of 1 medium orange

Juice of 1 medium orange

Zest of 1 medium lemon

Juice of 1 medium lemon

Zest of 1 medium lime

Juice of 1 medium lime

1. In a large skillet over high heat, heat olive oil. Add lamb shanks and sear on all sides for about 5 to 7 minutes.

2. In a medium bowl, combine carrots, celery, sweet onion, garlic, tomato paste, chicken broth, salt, orange zest, orange juice, lemon zest, lemon juice, lime zest, and lime juice.

3. Transfer seared lamb shanks to a 6- to 8-quart (5.5- to 7.5-liter) slow cooker and pour vegetable mixture over lamb.

4. Cover and cook on low for 8 hours.

5. Serve hot. Strain vegetables from braising liquid and use as a topping for lamb.

Variation: Add ½ cup red wine to the braising liquid for a punch of flavor.

A shank often weighs upward of 1 pound (450 grams), which can make for quite a large serving size. Butchers sometimes cut the shank in half for easier serving. If you feel the shank is too large, use a fork to shred the meat from the bone, and serve it in a large serving bowl with the strained vegetables and a little braising liquid.

Cooking on high is not recommended for this cut.

Chapter 7

Chicken Dishes

Versatile chicken is easy to prepare in the slow cooker, and because chicken is a lean meat, you can cook it on the high setting. Contrary to popular belief, poultry can easily dry out, even in the moisture-rich environment of the slow cooker. (Turkey is notorious for drying out. If you try turkey in a slow cooker, use a meat thermometer while cooking and closely monitor it because exact cooking times vary greatly among cuts and size.)

The chicken recipes in this chapter are intended for use in 6- to 8-quart (5.5- to 7.5-liter) slow cookers. The smaller end of this range uses the short end of the listed cooking times, while the larger slow cookers might require the entire range of time listed. The recipes, excluding the whole chicken, can all be doubled in a larger slow cooker. Note that bone-in chicken takes longer to cook than boneless.

Deliciously whole chicken is made right in the slow cooker for a faux rotisserie chicken you can prep and forget. Crusted with herbs and moistened by butter, this chicken is tender and moist.

Yield	2 or 3 pounds meat (1 to 1.5 kilograms)
Serving Size	1/3 pound (150 grams)
Prep Time	10 minutes
Cook Time	5 to 8 hours

1 (3- to 5-lb.; 1.5- to 2.5kg) whole chicken

1/4 cup butter

3 medium lemons

1 tsp. dried rosemary

1 tsp. dried oregano

1 tsp. dried basil

1 tsp. salt

1/2 tsp. black pepper

1. Remove and discard giblets and neck parts (if any) from cavity of chicken.

2. Using your finger, loosen skin on chicken by sliding it in at both ends. Divide butter into small pieces, and insert pieces in between skin and meat of chicken.

3. In a 6- to 8-quart (5.5- to 7.5-liter) slow cooker, place chicken, breast side down.

4. Cut lemons in half, and squeeze juice over chicken. Stuff squeezed lemon rinds into chicken cavity.

5. Sprinkle rosemary, oregano, basil, salt, and black pepper over chicken.

6. Cover and cook on low for 8 hours or high for 5 or 6 hours.

7. Remove lemon rinds from cavity and serve hot.

Variation: This chicken is easily adaptable by using different spices. For **Cajun Chicken,** for example, replace the rosemary, oregano, and basil with 1 tablespoon Cajun seasoning spice mix.

To avoid having the skin on the underside of the chicken melt in the juices, create a platform for the chicken to rest on. Simply crumble four large pieces of aluminum foil into balls, and place the balls on the bottom of the slow cooker. Set the chicken on top of the foil balls so it doesn't sits in any of the juices.

Herb-Roasted Whole Chicken

Honey Chipotle Barbecue Chicken Drumsticks

Tender drumsticks are simmered in a honey chipotle barbecue sauce. The chipotle brings both heat and smokiness to the homemade sauce.

Yield	12 drumsticks
Serving Size	2 drumsticks
Prep Time	5 minutes
Cook Time	4 to 8 hours

12 chicken drumsticks

½ cup ketchup

¼ cup brown sugar, firmly packed

¼ cup honey

1 chipotle chile in adobo sauce, finely chopped

2 tsp. apple cider vinegar

1½ tsp. Worcestershire sauce

½ tsp. garlic powder

¼ tsp. salt

1 pinch black pepper

1. In a 6- to 8-quart (5.5- to 7.5-liter) slow cooker, place chicken drumsticks.

2. In a small bowl, whisk together ketchup, brown sugar, honey, chipotle chile in adobo sauce, apple cider vinegar, Worcestershire sauce, garlic powder, salt, and black pepper.

3. Pour barbecue sauce over chicken.

4. Cover and cook on low for 6 to 8 hours or on high for 4 or 5 hours.

5. Serve hot.

Variation: You can use any bone-in chicken parts in place of the drumsticks. Thighs, wings, and bone-in chicken breasts are all suitable. Wings require the lower range of cooking time because they're small, while bone-in breasts require the maximum due to their larger size.

Chipotle chiles in adobo sauce are canned, smoked jalapeños. They have a distinct smoky flavor and are spicy, so recipes often call for only a small amount. You can store the leftovers in an airtight container, like a resealable plastic storage bag, and freeze them for later use.

To increase the heat, you can add more chipotle chiles to this recipe. Taste as you add the chiles to be sure you don't get it too hot.

Bite-size pieces of chicken are gently stewed in this sweet curry. The flavors of coconut and acidic tomatoes bring out the bright notes of the sauce.

Yield	6 cups
Serving Size	1 cup
Prep Time	5 minutes
Cook Time	4 to 8 hours

2 lb. (1kg) boneless, skinless chicken breasts, cut into 1-in. (2.5cm) cubes

½ large sweet onion, diced

4 cloves garlic, minced

1 (14-oz.; 400g) can coconut milk

1 (15-oz.; 420g) can diced tomatoes, drained

1 (8-oz.; 225g) can tomato sauce

2 TB. curry powder

1 TB. sugar

1 tsp. salt

1. In a 6- to 8-quart (5.5- to 7.5-liter) slow cooker, place chicken breasts, sweet onion, and garlic.

2. Pour in coconut milk, diced tomatoes, and tomato sauce.

3. Stir in curry powder, sugar, and salt.

4. Cover and cook on low for 6 to 8 hours or high for 4 or 5 hours.

5. Serve hot.

Variation: To increase the level of spiciness in the curry, add 1 teaspoon crushed red pepper flakes.

Not all curry powders are created equal. Curry powder is a spice mixture with no set ingredients or proportions. So every curry powder you buy will be different. Many curry blends found in the United States and other Western countries commonly contain coriander, fenugreek, red pepper, and turmeric. (Turmeric is the ingredient that gives curry powder its yellow coloring.) You can experiment with different brands of curry powder to find one to your liking.

Coconut Chicken Curry

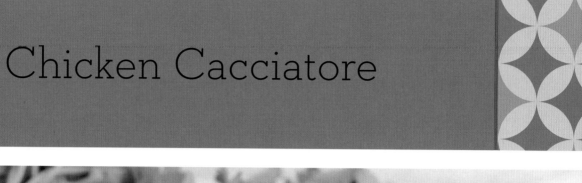

Chicken Cacciatore

Chicken breast is slow braised in a simmering sauce of tomatoes, onion, bell pepper, and herbs. The chicken is dredged and browned prior to slow cooking for an added depth of texture and flavor.

Yield	3 chicken breasts
Serving Size	½ breast
Prep Time	10 minutes
Cook Time	4 to 8 hours

1 cup all-purpose flour

1½ tsp. salt

1½ tsp. dried basil

1 tsp. paprika

1 tsp. black pepper

3 (½- to ¾-lb.; 225- to 340g) boneless, skinless chicken breasts, trimmed

2 TB. olive oil

1 medium yellow onion, diced

2 cloves garlic, minced

1 large green bell pepper, ribs and seeds removed, and diced

1 (15-oz.; 420g) can diced tomatoes, with juice

½ tsp. dried oregano

1. In a shallow bowl, stir together all-purpose flour, 1 teaspoon salt, 1 teaspoon basil, paprika, and ½ teaspoon black pepper.

2. Place chicken breasts in flour mixture, and turn to coat each side.

3. In a large skillet over medium-high heat, heat olive oil. Add chicken and sear for 3 minutes per side. Transfer cooked chicken to a 6- to 8-quart (5.5- to 7.5-liter) slow cooker.

4. Add yellow onion, garlic, green bell pepper, tomatoes with juice, remaining ½ teaspoon salt, remaining ½ teaspoon basil, remaining ½ teaspoon black pepper, and oregano to the slow cooker.

5. Cover and cook on high for 4 or 5 hours or on low for 6 to 8 hours.

6. Serve hot, topped with sauce.

Variation: When ready to serve, heat a large skillet over high heat. Add 1 tablespoon olive oil and 8 ounces (225 grams) sliced button mushrooms. Cook, stirring occasionally, for 5 minutes. Serve mushrooms on top of hot chicken.

Cacciatore is an Italian word that translates to "hunter." It refers to cooking a dish hunter style, which includes tomatoes, onions, herbs, and bell peppers.

A sweet, soy-based glaze thickens in the slow cooker and soaks into tender chicken breasts for a succulent and flavorful version of the classic Japanese-inspired dish.

Yield	3 chicken breasts
Serving Size	½ breast
Prep Time	5 minutes
Cook Time	4 to 8 hours

3 (½- to ¾-lb.; 225- to 340g) boneless, skinless chicken breasts, trimmed

1 TB. cornstarch

½ cup sugar

½ tsp. ground ginger

¼ tsp. crushed red pepper flakes

½ cup soy sauce

¼ cup rice vinegar

2 cloves garlic, minced

1. In a 6- to 8-quart (5.5- to 7.5-liter) slow cooker, place chicken breasts.

2. In a small bowl, whisk together cornstarch, sugar, ginger, and crushed red pepper flakes.

3. Whisk in soy sauce, rice vinegar, and garlic. Pour glaze over chicken.

4. Cover and cook on low for 6 to 8 hours or high for 4 or 5 hours.

5. Slice and serve hot with rice.

Variation: You can use 2 pounds (1 kilogram) whole chicken thighs, 2 pounds (1 kilogram) drumsticks, or 2 pounds (1 kilogram) wings in place of chicken breasts. Serve with glaze drizzled over top.

Cornstarch is used as a thickening agent in this recipe. If mixed with liquid on its own, it can cause lumps to form. If you mix the fine-powdered cornstarch with the sugar and spices beforehand, it can easily incorporate into the sauce without clumping together.

Teriyaki Chicken

Chicken Tikka Masala

Tender chunks of chicken are simmered in a spicy, tomato-based sauce and flavored with garam masala. Heavy cream gives this sensational sauce an added richness.

Yield	6 cups
Serving Size	1 cup
Prep Time	5 minutes
Cook Time	4 to 8 hours

2 lb. (1kg) boneless, skinless chicken breasts, cut into 1-in. (2.5cm) cubes

3 cloves garlic, minced

1 jalapeño, stem removed, and minced

1 TB. paprika

2 tsp. cumin

2 tsp. garam masala

2 (8-oz.; 225g) cans tomato sauce

2 TB. tomato paste

1½ tsp. salt

1 cup heavy whipping cream

½ cup chopped fresh cilantro

1. In a 6- to 8-quart (5.5- to 7.5-liter) slow cooker, place chicken breasts.

2. Stir in garlic, jalapeño, paprika, cumin, garam masala, tomato sauce, tomato paste, and salt.

3. Cover and cook on low for 6 to 8 hours or on high for 4 or 5 hours.

4. When ready to serve, stir in heavy whipping cream and garnish with cilantro.

Tikka is a word used in Indian and Pakistani cuisine to denote chunks of meat in a spice marinade. You can use this same sauce mixture over lamb or the Indian cheese paneer, or make a vegetable version using cauliflower.

Garam masala is an Indian spice mixture of cumin, coriander, cardamom, black pepper, cinnamon, cloves, and nutmeg. The whole spices are toasted and ground into a distinctly flavorful mixture. Garam masala is sold in the spice section of most grocery stores.

A sweet orange sauce envelopes bite-size pieces of chicken for a slow cooked version of the popular restaurant dish.

Yield   3 cups

Serving Size   ½ cup

Prep Time   5 minutes

Cook Time   4 to 8 hours

2 lb. (1kg) boneless, skinless chicken breasts, trimmed

1 medium orange

⅓ cup brown sugar, firmly packed

1 tsp. cornstarch

1 tsp. ground ginger

1 tsp. crushed red pepper flakes

1 cup orange juice

¼ cup rice vinegar

2 TB. soy sauce

1. Cut chicken breasts into bite-size pieces, and place in a 6- to 8-quart (5.5- to 7.5-liter) slow cooker.

2. Using a zester or a small grater, zest orange. You need about 1 or 2 tablespoons zest. Set aside zest.

3. Slice orange into ¼-inch (6.5-millimeter) slices. Set aside.

4. In a small bowl, whisk together brown sugar, cornstarch, ginger, and crushed red pepper flakes.

5. Whisk in orange juice, orange zest, rice vinegar, and soy sauce. Pour sauce over chicken, and place orange slices on top.

6. Cover and cook on low for 6 to 8 hours or on high for 4 or 5 hours.

7. When ready to serve, discard orange slices, and serve chicken hot over rice.

Variation: Use 2 pounds (1 kilogram) whole chicken thighs, 2 pounds (1 kilogram) drumsticks, or 2 pounds (1 kilogram) wings in place of chicken breasts. Serve them whole with orange glaze drizzled over top.

Topping the chicken with orange slices not only uses the flesh of the orange after zesting, but also helps keep any exposed chicken moist and infuses the sauce with even more sweet orange flavor.

Orange Chicken

Moroccan Chicken Thighs

These chicken thighs are cooked between beds of tart and tangy lemon slices and coated with a bold, Moroccan-style spice mixture. The lemon and butter ensure a moist and tender piece of chicken.

Yield	6 thighs
Serving Size	1 thigh
Prep Time	5 minutes
Cook Time	4 to 8 hours

2 medium lemons, sliced ⅛ in. (3.18mm) thick

6 chicken thighs

1 tsp. paprika

½ tsp. cumin

¼ tsp. turmeric

¼ tsp. cayenne

¼ tsp. salt

⅛ tsp. ground cinnamon

⅛ tsp. ground ginger

3 TB. butter

1. In a 6- to 8-quart (5.5- to 7.5-liter) slow cooker, layer half of lemon slices. Place chicken thighs on top.

2. In a small bowl, combine paprika, cumin, turmeric, cayenne, salt, cinnamon, and ginger. Sprinkle over chicken thighs.

3. Cut butter into 6 (½-tablespoon) pieces, and place 1 piece on top of each chicken thigh.

4. Cover and cook on low for 6 to 8 hours or high for 4 or 5 hours.

5. Serve hot.

Variation: For **Mexican-Spiced Chicken,** use 4 limes in place of the lemons. Instead of spices listed in step 2, use 2 teaspoons cumin, 1 teaspoon chili powder, ½ teaspoon cayenne, ½ teaspoon garlic powder, ½ teaspoon salt, and ⅛ teaspoon ground cloves.

For a crispy skin on the chicken, remove the lemon slices after cooking and place the chicken on a baking sheet. Place under an oven broiler preheated to high for 2 to 5 minutes or until the skin is crispy. Watch carefully to avoid burning.

Layers of creamy green chile chicken and flour tortillas are slow cooked casserole-style. Add some melted cheese, and you have a rich and decadent "enchilada" dinner, slow cooker style.

Yield	**8 slices**
Serving Size	**1 slice**
Prep Time	**15 minutes**
Cook Time	**4 to 8 hours**

4 TB. butter

2 cloves garlic, minced

⅓ cup all-purpose flour

1 tsp. chili powder

1 tsp. cumin

1 tsp. salt

2 cups chicken broth

4 cups chicken, cooked and shredded

1 medium yellow onion, diced

1 cup sour cream

2 (4-oz.; 110g) cans diced green chiles, with liquid

10 (7½-in.; 20cm) flour tortillas

2 cups shredded Monterey jack cheese

1. In a medium saucepan over low heat, melt butter. Increase heat to medium, add garlic, and cook for 60 seconds.

2. Whisk in all-purpose flour, chili powder, cumin, and salt to form a paste.

3. Pour in chicken broth, increase heat to high, and whisk until broth reaches a simmer and thickens. Remove from heat, and transfer broth to a large bowl.

4. Add chicken, yellow onion, sour cream, and green chiles with liquid to broth, and stir to combine.

5. Set aside about ¼ cup sauce.

6. Place 2 tortillas in the bottom of a 6- to 8-quart (5.5- to 7.5-liter) oval slow cooker, overlapping them in the middle. If you're using a round slow cooker, only use 1 tortilla in each layer.

7. Top tortilla(s) with ¼ chicken mixture, and top chicken with ¼ cup Monterey jack cheese. Repeat layering with 4 chicken layers. Top last layer with final layer of tortilla(s), and spread reserved 2 spoonfuls sauce over last layer, just enough to wet tortillas. Top with remaining 1 cup cheese.

8. Cover and cook on high for 4 or 5 hours or on low for 6 to 8 hours.

9. Cut into 8 slices and serve hot as is, or topped with a dollop of sour cream and chopped fresh cilantro if desired.

Green Chile Chicken Enchilada Casserole

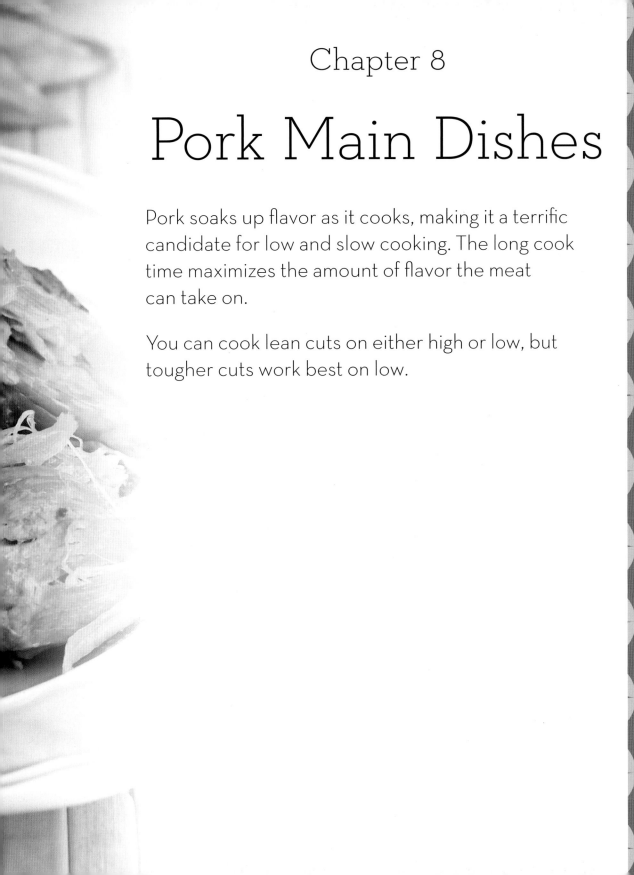

Chapter 8

Pork Main Dishes

Pork soaks up flavor as it cooks, making it a terrific candidate for low and slow cooking. The long cook time maximizes the amount of flavor the meat can take on.

You can cook lean cuts on either high or low, but tougher cuts work best on low.

Apple Pork Roast

Sweet apples and onions surround supple pork in this slow cooked roast that highlights the flavors of fall.

Yield	3 or 4 pounds (1.5 to 2 kilograms) pork
Serving Size	½ to ⅓ pound (115 to 150 grams) pork
Prep Time	5 minutes
Cook Time	6 to 8 hours

1 (3- or 4-lb.; 1.5- to 2kg) pork roast

4 medium apples, cored, halved, and quartered

½ cup apple juice

2 TB. brown sugar

1 tsp. salt

1 large sweet onion, halved and sliced

1. In a 6- to 8-quart (5.5- to 7.5-liter) slow cooker, place pork roast.

2. Surround roast with apples, and pour apple juice over top.

3. Sprinkle brown sugar and salt over roast, and top with sweet onion.

4. Cover and cook on low for 6 to 8 hours.

5. Slice and serve hot with apples and onions.

Variation: You can use 4 bone-in thick-cut pork chops in place of the roast in this recipe. The cook time is the same.

You have many choices when it comes to pork roasts. Pork loin and sirloin roasts are leaner cuts that won't shred as easily, allowing you to slice the roast to serve it. Shoulder and butt roasts are marbled with fat and will shred easily after a long, slow cooking process.

These tender, fall-off-the-bone ribs are sure to please any meat lover. The strawberry-chipotle barbecue sauce stews with the meat for a succulent, sweet, and spicy bite of delicate, juicy meat.

Yield	2 racks
Serving Size	½ rack
Prep Time	20 minutes
Cook Time	8 hours

2 TB. olive oil

1 large sweet onion, diced

2 cloves garlic, minced

2 cups strawberries, hulled

3 chipotle chiles in adobo sauce

1 cup ketchup

⅔ cup brown sugar, tightly packed

1 TB. Worcestershire sauce

2 tsp. ground mustard

½ tsp. black pepper

2 racks pork loin baby back ribs

1. In a large saucepan over medium-high heat, heat olive oil. Add sweet onion, and sauté, stirring occasionally, for 5 minutes.

2. Add garlic and sauté for 60 seconds.

3. Stir in strawberries, chipotle chiles, ketchup, brown sugar, Worcestershire sauce, ground mustard, and black pepper. Increase heat to high and bring to a boil. Reduce heat to medium-low and simmer for 10 minutes.

4. Transfer to a blender or a food processor fitted with an S blade, and blend until smooth.

5. In a 6- to 8-quart (5.5- to 7.5-liter) slow cooker, place ribs. If racks are too large to fit in your slow cooker, cut them in half. Pour sauce over ribs.

6. Cover and cook on low for 8 hours.

7. Serve hot.

Variation: You can use any barbecue sauce you like in this recipe, including the others included in this book.

Give slow cooked ribs that extra "grilled" touch by brushing the cooked ribs with additional barbecue sauce and placing them under a broiler for a few minutes until the sauce caramelizes, bubbles, and darkens. Or brush them with the extra sauce, wrap them in aluminum foil, and place them on an outdoor grill for 5 to 7 minutes.

Strawberry-Chipotle Barbecue Baby Back Ribs

Dijon-Crusted Pork Tenderloin

The concentrated, tangy flavors of Dijon mustard form a flavorful crust on this cut of tenderloin.

Yield	8 slices
Serving Size	2 or 3 slices
Prep Time	5 minutes
Cook Time	3 to 7 hours

1 (1-lb.; 450g) pork tenderloin

½ tsp. salt

¼ tsp. black pepper

2 TB. Dijon mustard

1. Season pork tenderloin with salt and black pepper.

2. Rub outside of tenderloin with Dijon mustard, and place tenderloin in a 6- to 8-quart (5.5- to 7.5-liter) slow cooker.

3. Cover and cook on high for 3 or 4 hours or on low for 5 to 7 hours.

4. Let tenderloin rest for 10 minutes.

5. Slice into ½-inch (1-centimeter) slices, and serve hot.

Variation: For a spicy crusted tenderloin, coat the outside of the meat with 2 tablespoons chipotle chili powder (or 3 chipotle chiles in adobo sauce, minced), ½ teaspoon garlic powder, ½ teaspoon onion powder, ½ teaspoon salt, and 2 tablespoons brown sugar for a sweet note.

Pork tenderloins are quite small, so you can easily double this recipe. Lay the tenderloins in a single layer, side by side in the slow cooker, and cook as directed.

This slow cooker version of the island favorite is tender and moist. The liquid smoke provides the deep pit-smoked flavor, and the salt brings an island taste of the sea.

Yield	3 or 4 pounds (1.5 to 2 kilograms) pork
Serving Size	¼ to ⅓ pound (115 to 150 grams) pork
Prep Time	5 minutes
Cook Time	8 hours

1 (3- or 4-lb.; 1.5- to 2kg) boneless pork butt or shoulder roast

3 TB. liquid smoke

1 TB. sea salt

1. In a 6- to 8-quart (5.5- to 7.5-liter) slow cooker, place pork roast.

2. Pour liquid smoke over roast, and season with sea salt.

3. Cover and cook on low 8 hours.

4. Shred meat with a fork, and serve hot.

Variation: For a more authentic flavor, use Hawaiian pink salt, if you have access to it.

Kalua refers to a traditional Hawaiian cooking method in which food is cooked in an underground oven. Hot rocks are used as a heat source, and banana leaves provide a lining. The heat is low, the cooking process is long—much like slow cooking—and the item being cooked soaks up a smoky flavor during the process. You can enjoy kalua pork many ways. Eat it plain with rice and/or traditional Hawaiian accompaniments like poi or poke. Hawaiian sweet rolls are often used to make a kalua sandwich.

Hawaiian Kalua Pork

Killer Carnitas

This tender, shredded pork packs a bold flavor, thanks to the cumin and chili powder, and the cayenne brings just enough heat to add a little kick. Cooked in vegetable oil, this meat is ultratender and indulgent.

Yield	6 cups
Serving Size	½ cup
Prep Time	10 minutes
Cook Time	6 to 8 hours

4 lb. (2kg) pork butt roast

2 TB. ground cumin

1 TB. chili powder

2 tsp. garlic powder

2 tsp. salt

1½ tsp. cayenne

1 tsp. ground cloves

2 cups vegetable oil

2 bay leaves

1. Trim pork roast of excess fat and slice into ¼-inch-thick (.5-centimeter) pieces, discarding any large deposits of fat. Place trimmed meat in a 6- to 8-quart (5.5- to 7.5-liter) slow cooker.

2. In a medium bowl, combine cumin, chili powder, garlic powder, salt, cayenne, cloves, and vegetable oil.

3. Pour spiced oil over pork roast and stir to coat. Tuck bay leaves down into oil.

4. Cover and cook on low for 6 to 8 hours or until meat is easily shredded with a fork.

5. Strain oil from meat, remove bay leaves, and shred meat completely before serving.

Variation: Add ½ cup orange juice with vegetable oil for a regional variation of carnitas.

Carnitas, or "little meats," is a popular Mexican braised pork. You can serve the tender, shredded meat as a dish by itself, or use it in tacos, burritos, tamales, or tortas. You don't need much to dress up this flavorful meat. A taco only needs some fresh cilantro, diced onion, and diced tomato on a corn or flour tortilla to bring a big, bold taco bite.

Making a delicious ham couldn't be any easier than this vibrant, tangy, and sweet glazed ham.

Yield	2 or 3 servings per 1 pound (450 grams)
Serving Size	⅓ to ½ pound (150 to 225 grams)
Prep Time	5 minutes
Cook Time	5 to 8 hours

1 (5- to 8-lb.; 2.5- to 4kg) fully cooked bone-in smoked ham

1 cup orange juice

½ cup balsamic vinegar

½ cup brown sugar, tightly packed

1 tsp. salt

1. In a 6- to 8-quart (5.5- to 7.5-liter) slow cooker, place ham, cut side down.

2. In a medium bowl, stir together orange juice, balsamic vinegar, brown sugar, and salt. Pour glaze over ham.

3. Cover and cook on low for 5 to 8 hours or approximately 1 hour per 1 pound (450 grams) ham.

4. Serve hot.

It's important to ensure the ham you buy fits in your slow cooker. There's no shame in bringing a small measuring tape with you to the grocery store to measure the hams before you buy one. The slow cooker lid must be able to rest securely on the rim of the stoneware insert, so plan accordingly.

Orange-Balsamic
Glazed Ham

Smothered Pork Chops

Flavorful gravy and cooked onions provide the "smothering" gravy for these thick and tender pork chops. Spoon on the gravy for a saucy pork dinner.

Yield	4 chops
Serving Size	1 chop
Prep Time	5 minutes
Cook Time	4 to 8 hours

4 (½- to 1-in.; 1- to 2.5cm thick) bone-in pork chops

1 tsp. salt

½ tsp. black pepper

1 TB. cornstarch

1 TB. water

1 cup chicken broth

2 tsp. onion powder

2 tsp. garlic powder

2 large sweet onions, halved and sliced

1. Season both sides of pork chops with salt and black pepper. Place chops in a 6- to 8-quart (5.5- to 7.5-liter) slow cooker.

2. In a small bowl, combine cornstarch and water.

3. Stir cornstarch mixture into chicken broth, and stir in onion powder and garlic powder. Pour gravy around pork chops in the slow cooker.

4. Top chops with sweet onions.

5. Cover and cook on high for 4 or 5 hours or on low for 6 to 8 hours.

6. Serve hot, smothered with gravy and onions.

Bone-in pork chops are preferable to boneless in this recipe because they're harder to dry out. The bone helps the meat retain moisture and slows the cooking process, resulting in a moist and tender slow cooked chop.

Chapter 9

Versatile Vegetables

In addition to softening tough cuts of meat, the slow cooker can transform vegetables that require long cooking times like artichokes and potatoes. With a slow cooker and a few hours, you'll get delicious vegetable dishes that are sure to please.

Get the gourmet feel of stuffed artichokes with the help of the slow cooker. Seasoned breadcrumbs and Parmesan cheese fill the interior of the artichokes, topping the heart with buttery goodness.

Yield	4 artichokes
Serving Size	1 artichoke
Prep Time	15 minutes
Cook Time	3 to 6 hours

4 large whole artichokes

1 cup breadcrumbs

1 cup shredded Parmesan cheese

4 cloves garlic, minced

1 tsp. dried basil

¼ tsp. salt

½ cup butter, melted

1. Cut off stems of artichokes so they sit upright. Trim off any sharp leaf tips using a pair of kitchen scissors.

2. Using a large spoon, scoop out and discard artichoke center chokes, or hairs.

3. In a medium bowl, combine breadcrumbs, Parmesan cheese, garlic, basil, and salt. Stir in melted butter.

4. Evenly divide breadcrumb mixture among artichokes, and spoon into hollowed-out centers.

5. Pour water into the bottom of a 6- to 8-quart (5.5- to 7.5-liter) slow cooker, enough to cover the bottom by ½ inch (1 centimeter). Stand artichokes in water.

6. Cover and cook on low for 5 to 6 hours or on high for 3 or 4 hours.

7. To eat, scoop down through breadcrumb mixture to heart so you enjoy a spoonful of both stuffing and artichoke. As you make your way to the center heart, peel back and eat flesh from tips of leaves by scraping it off with your teeth.

Variation: Add ½ cup chopped sun-dried tomatoes to the breadcrumb mixture.

The artichokes might turn brown a bit after you hollow out the centers. To prevent this, rub the exposed artichoke heart with a little lemon juice immediately after cutting.

Stuffed Artichokes

Country-Style Green Beans

The low and slow method a slow cooker offers produces soft and tender green beans, smothered in onion, with just a hint of smoky ham.

Yield	6 cups
Serving Size	1 cup
Prep Time	10 minutes
Cook Time	6 to 8 hours

1½ lb. (680g) fresh green beans, ends trimmed

1 medium yellow onion, diced

½ tsp. salt

6 cloves garlic, minced

¼ tsp. crushed red pepper flakes

¼ tsp. black pepper

1 (8-oz.; 225g) ham hock

1. In a 4- to 6-quart (4- to 5.5-liter) slow cooker, toss together green beans, yellow onion, salt, garlic, crushed red pepper flakes, and black pepper.

2. Using a knife, make several slashes across surface of ham hock. Add ham to the slow cooker, burrowing it down into green beans.

3. Cover and cook on low for 6 to 8 hours.

4. Remove and discard ham hock before serving green beans.

Variation: For a vegetarian version, you can omit the ham hock.

When purchasing fresh green beans, avoid beans that are shriveled or limp. To prepare them for cooking, either snap or trim off the ends and discard them. You can then either snap the beans in half or leave them long.

Collard greens get a low and slow treatment in this spicy dish. The southern leafy greens are slowly simmered in a flavorful broth until the leaves are tasty and tender.

Yield	3 cups
Serving Size	½ cup
Prep Time	5 minutes
Cook Time	2 to 6 hours

1 lb. (450g) collard greens, stems removed and roughly chopped

1 medium yellow onion, diced

2 cloves garlic, minced

1 tsp. salt

½ tsp. black pepper

½ tsp. crushed red pepper flakes

3 cups chicken broth

1. In a 4- to 6-quart (4- to 5.5-liter) slow cooker, combine collard greens, yellow onion, garlic, salt, black pepper, and crushed red pepper flakes.

2. Pour in chicken broth.

3. Cover and cook on high for 2 or 3 hours or on low for 4 to 6 hours.

Variation: For a smoky ham flavor, add a ham hock to the slow cooker while cooking. Remove and discard it before serving.

Collard greens are in the same family as cabbage and broccoli. The leaves are quite thick, which means they need a long cook time to become tender. The stems, although edible, are particularly tough and can end up chewy. To remove the stems, simply use a sharp knife to cut them out.

Southern Collard Greens

Corn on the Cob

Summertime corn on the cob has never been easier. Simply season, wrap, and cook, and you get sweet, butter-soaked corn that's ready to eat right out of the slow cooker.

Yield	6 ears
Serving Size	1 ear
Prep Time	10 minutes
Cook Time	2 to 5 hours

6 medium ears corn, shucked

6 TB. butter, softened

½ tsp. salt

½ tsp. black pepper

1. Tear off 6 (12-inch; 15-centimeter) pieces of aluminum foil.

2. Place 1 ear of corn on each piece of aluminum foil.

3. Smear 1 tablespoon softened butter over each ear of corn, and season corn with salt and black pepper.

4. Wrap up each ear tightly in the foil, and place wrapped ears in a 6- to 8-quart (5.5- to 7.5-liter) slow cooker.

5. Cover and cook on high for 2 or 3 hours or on low for 4 or 5 hours.

Variation: This recipe is easy to change with almost any seasoning. For **Chili and Lime Corn on the Cob,** season each buttered cob with ½ teaspoon chili powder and squeeze lime juice over top before wrapping. For **Curry Corn on the Cob,** season each buttered cob with ½ teaspoon curry powder and ⅛ teaspoon salt before wrapping. For **Coconut Lime Corn on the Cob,** brush each cob with 1 tablespoon melted coconut oil instead of butter and then squeeze lime juice over each cob before wrapping. For **Mexican Street Corn on the Cob,** combine ¼ cup mayonnaise, ¼ cup sour cream, ½ cup crumbled feta or cotija cheese, ½ teaspoon chili powder, and 2 cloves crushed garlic, and spread mixture over each cob before wrapping.

When choosing ears of corn, look for ones with bright green husks. Peel back a little of the husk, exposing just the tip of the cob, to check the corn kernels. The kernels should have a fresh yellow or white color and be nice and plump. Avoid ears with dry or discolored kernels.

In this easy, slow cooked corn dish, with its creamy texture and sweet taste, creamed corn becomes a decadent treat.

Yield	6 cups
Serving Size	½ cup
Prep Time	5 minutes
Cook Time	2 or 3 hours

6 cups frozen corn kernels, thawed

1 cup milk

1 TB. sugar

½ tsp. salt

8 oz. (225g) cream cheese

½ cup butter

1. In a 4- to 6-quart (4- to 5.5-liter) slow cooker, combine corn, milk, sugar, and salt.

2. Cut cream cheese and butter into ½-inch (1.25-centimeter) cubes, and place on top of corn.

3. Cover and cook on high for 2 or 3 hours.

4. Stir before serving hot.

Why wait 2 or 3 hours for this recipe to cook when you can just open a can of cream corn? The two are quite different. Canned cream-style corn is partially puréed to create a soupy sweet corn mixture with the "milk," or juice from the corn. With this recipe, plenty of butter and cream cheese combine for a truly decadent cream base for the sweet corn.

Creamed Corn

Ratatouille

This version of the traditional French dish slow cooks fresh and flavorful veggies to delicious goodness with very little additional flavoring. Garlic, salt, and pepper are enough to showcase the natural flavors of the vegetables.

Yield	6 cups
Serving Size	1 cup
Prep Time	15 minutes
Cook Time	2 to 5 hours

1 medium eggplant, peeled and diced

1 medium zucchini, diced

1 large green bell pepper, ribs and seeds removed, and diced

2 medium tomatoes, hulled and diced

1 medium yellow onion, diced

1 (8-oz.; 225g) can tomato sauce

4 cloves garlic, minced

1 tsp. salt

½ tsp. black pepper

1. In a 4- to 6-quart (4- to 5.5-liter) slow cooker, combine eggplant, zucchini, green bell pepper, tomatoes, yellow onion, tomato sauce, garlic, salt, and black pepper.

2. Cover and cook on high for 2 or 3 hours or on low for 4 or 5 hours.

Variation: Instead of dicing the ingredients, you could slice them thinly and create a layered version of the dish, alternating slices of the various vegetables.

Ratatouille is usually served as a side dish, but it also can be a main dish, especially when accompanied by bread or pasta. You could use it as a crostini topping, too. Simply top a slice of a crusty French loaf bread with a spoonful of ratatouille. You can even add a bit of shredded Parmesan cheese on top and toast it under a broiler for a few minutes, just until browned.

These summer vegetables have a smoky, straight-off-the-grill flavor, thanks to liquid smoke. This super-easy side is perfect for a summer barbecue or picnic.

Yield	4 cups
Serving Size	¾ cup
Prep Time	5 minutes
Cook Time	2 to 4 hours

1 pt. (470ml) cherry tomatoes

1 medium zucchini, ends removed, halved, and sliced

1 medium yellow onion, cut into 1-in. (2.5cm) chunks

2 large red bell peppers, ribs and stems removed, and cut into 1-in. (2.5cm) chunks

½ tsp. salt

¼ tsp. black pepper

2 TB. olive oil

1 tsp. liquid smoke

1. In a 3- to 6-quart (3- to 5.5-liter) slow cooker, combine cherry tomatoes, zucchini, yellow onion, and red bell peppers.

2. Season with salt and black pepper, pour in olive oil and liquid smoke, and stir to coat.

3. Cover and cook on high for 2 hours or on low for 3 or 4 hours or just until vegetables are tender.

Zucchini is abundant during the summer months, and home gardeners often give it away to friends and neighbors by the bushel. The thick stem on the top end of the zucchini is inedible and should be cut off. You can leave on the skins or peel them off. It's better that the skins be left on for slow cooking because the thick skin holds the soft flesh together.

Roasted Summer Vegetable Medley

Cheesy Bacon and Ranch Potatoes

Potatoes coated with the spices of traditional ranch dressing and topped with bacon make a delicious dish you'll love. Cheese and buttermilk finish it off for a creamy and flavorful potato side.

Yield	6 cups
Serving Size	1 cup
Prep Time	15 minutes
Cook Time	3 to 7 hours

1 lb. (450g) bacon

8 medium red potatoes, cut into 1-in. (2.5cm) cubes

1 medium yellow onion, diced

1 TB. dried parsley

1 tsp. dried dill

1 tsp. salt

½ tsp. garlic powder

½ tsp. onion powder

½ tsp. dried chives

¼ tsp. black pepper

2 TB. olive oil

2 cups shredded cheddar cheese

½ cup buttermilk

½ cup sliced green onions, green parts only

1. Place bacon in a room-temperature skillet, set over medium heat, and cook for 10 minutes. Flip over bacon and cook for 7 to 10 more minutes or until bacon is crispy. Transfer bacon to a paper towel–covered plate to drain.

2. In a 6- to 8-quart (5.5- to 7.5-liter) slow cooker, combine red potatoes, yellow onion, parsley, dill, salt, garlic powder, onion powder, chives, black pepper, and olive oil.

3. Crumble cooked bacon over top of potato mixture.

4. Cover and cook on high for 3 or 4 hours or on low for 6 or 7 hours or until potatoes are tender.

5. Stir cheddar cheese and buttermilk into hot potatoes, top with green onions, and serve hot.

Variation: You can omit the bacon for a vegetarian-friendly version.

Starting the bacon in a cold pan lets the fat loosen up and ensures the bacon cooks more evenly. Adding bacon to a hot pan can result in scorching. Cooking bacon until crisp before adding it to the slow cooker keeps the bacon from getting too soggy during the slow cooking process. In this dish, the bacon is crumbled over the top so it doesn't get additional cooking time down in liquids where it would become soggy. Keeping the bacon up on top helps it remain crisp.

Cheesy Bacon and Ranch Potatoes   185

In this buttery honey mustard potato dish, red potatoes are coated in the acidic and slightly spicy flavors of Dijon mustard. Honey adds a nice, sweet note.

Yield   6 cups

Serving Size   1 cup

Prep Time   10 minutes

Cook Time   3 to 7 hours

8 medium red potatoes, cut into 1-in. (2.5cm) pieces

1 medium yellow onion, diced

¼ cup butter

¼ cup honey

1 TB. Dijon mustard

1 tsp. dried oregano

1 tsp. salt

½ tsp. black pepper

1. In a 6- to 8-quart (5.5- to 7.5-liter) slow cooker, combine red potatoes, yellow onion, butter, honey, Dijon mustard, oregano, salt, and black pepper.

2. Cover and cook on high for 3 or 4 hours or on low for 6 or 7 hours or until potatoes are tender.

3. Stir and serve hot.

Does it really matter what kind of onion you use in this recipe? Yes ... and no. Yellow onions and sweet onions are the most versatile, and both work really well in the slow cooker. Yellow onions produce a mild onion flavor after the slow cooking process, sweet onions produce a mild onion flavor plus a slightly sweet note, and white onions produce a sharper onion flavor and don't soften as much. Red onions are best eaten raw.

Honey Mustard-Roasted Potatoes

Creamy Whipped Potatoes

Butter, buttermilk, and cream cheese add to the flavor and creaminess of these slow cooker mashed potatoes that are whipped to a deliciously smooth texture.

Yield	2 cups
Serving Size	1 cup
Prep Time	10 minutes
Cook Time	4 to 7 hours

5 large russet potatoes, peeled and cubed

6 cups chicken broth

½ cup butter

8 oz. (225g) cream cheese

1 cup buttermilk

1½ tsp. salt

¼ cup green onions, green parts only, sliced (optional)

1. In a 6- to 8-quart (5.5- to 7.5-liter) slow cooker, place russet potatoes.

2. Pour in chicken broth.

3. Cover and cook on low for 5 or 6 hours or on high 3 or 4 hours or until potatoes are tender.

4. Drain excess liquid from potatoes.

5. Using an electric mixer on high speed, whip potatoes for about 2 minutes in the slow cooker.

6. Add butter, cream cheese, buttermilk, and salt on top of potatoes.

7. Cover and cook on high for 1 more hour to allow butter and cream cheese to melt.

8. Whip potatoes for 30 seconds, garnish with green onions (if using), and serve.

Variation: For **Garlic Whipped Potatoes,** add 4 cloves garlic, minced, with the butter.

Whipping the potatoes instead of mashing them produces a much smoother texture with little to no chunks. The cream cheese and butter in this recipe help create a smooth and creamy texture.

Thin-sliced potatoes bask in a creamy sauce enhanced by the earthy flavor of nutmeg. The slow cooker is the perfect cooking tool for this tender and creamy potato classic.

Yield	6 cups
Serving Size	1 cup
Prep Time	10 minutes
Cook Time	3 to 8 hours

2 large russet potatoes, peeled

1 cup heavy cream

2 cloves garlic, minced

½ cup freshly grated Parmesan cheese

½ tsp. ground nutmeg

½ tsp. salt

¼ tsp. black pepper

1. Slice russet potatoes into thin slices approximately ⅛ inch (3 millimeters) thick. Place slices in a large bowl.

2. Pour heavy cream over potatoes, and gently stir in garlic, Parmesan cheese, nutmeg, salt, and black pepper to coat potatoes.

3. Pour potatoes into a 6- to 8-quart (5.5- to 7.5-liter) slow cooker.

4. Cover and cook on low for 6 to 8 hours or on high for 3 or 4 hours.

Variation: For extra cheesiness, add 1 cup grated cheddar cheese on top during the last hour of cooking.

The easiest way to slice or scallop potatoes is using a food processor. It can take less than a minute to scallop the potatoes for this recipe. A mandoline is also handy and easily creates thin, even slices. If you don't have either of these tools, try using the slicing side of a cheese grater, rubbing the potatoes against the slicer for thin slices. A knife is the most difficult tool to use because slicing potatoes thin enough to be scalloped requires a very sharp knife and precision.

Scalloped Potatoes

Sweet Potato Casserole

Buttery sweet potatoes are seasoned with sugar and vanilla extract and topped with a pecan streusel. The combination of crunchy crust and creamy whipped sweet potatoes makes this a favorite almost-dessert side dish.

Yield	6 cups
Serving Size	1 cup
Prep Time	15 minutes
Cook Time	5 to 8 hours

6 medium sweet potatoes, peeled and cubed

6 cups water

½ cup sugar

½ tsp. salt

4 TB. butter

½ cup milk

½ tsp. vanilla extract

½ cup brown sugar, firmly packed

⅓ cup all-purpose flour

3 TB. butter, softened

½ cup chopped pecans

1. In a 6- to 8-quart (5.5- to 7.5-liter) slow cooker, place sweet potatoes. Pour in water.

2. Cover and cook on high for 3 or 4 hours or low for 5 or 6 hours.

3. Drain excess liquid from sweet potatoes.

4. Using an electric mixer on high speed, whip potatoes for about 2 minutes or until smooth. Whip in sugar, salt, butter, milk, and vanilla extract.

5. Smooth whipped sweet potatoes into the bottom of the slow cooker.

6. In a small bowl, and using a pastry cutter, cut together brown sugar, all-purpose flour, and butter until mixture resembles cornmeal. Stir in chopped pecans, and sprinkle pecan mixture over sweet potatoes.

7. Cover and cook on high for 2 hours.

8. Serve hot.

A pastry cutter is a handheld kitchen tool consisting of several strips of parallel metal or blades attached to a handle. It's most often used to cut fat into flour. If you don't have a pastry cutter, you can use two butter knives instead. Hold one butter knife in each hand with the tips in the dough, crossed near the handles. Quickly cut the knives parallel to each other, moving them in opposite directions. Repeat quickly, moving throughout the dough, cutting the butter into the flour and, in this recipe, the brown sugar.

The sweetness of fresh beets, sweet potatoes, and sweet onions combine in this savory side. Garlic and black pepper counteract the sweetness, making this a memorable dish.

Yield	6 cups
Serving Size	1 cup
Prep Time	15 minutes
Cook Time	3 to 7 hours

3 medium fresh beets, tops removed, peeled, and cubed

3 medium sweet potatoes, peeled and cubed

1 large sweet onion, diced

2 TB. olive oil

1 TB. brown sugar

1 tsp. garlic powder

1 tsp. salt

½ tsp. black pepper

1. In a 6- to 8-quart (5.5- to 7.5-liter) slow cooker, combine beets, sweet potatoes, and sweet onion.

2. Pour in olive oil, and stir in brown sugar, garlic powder, salt, and black pepper.

3. Cover and cook on high for 3 or 4 hours or high for 6 or 7 hours or until potatoes and beets are tender.

Fresh beets will stain everything they touch. Pink hands and cutting boards are common after cooking beets, as are stained shirts. Most stains can be rinsed away easily, but some people have been known to have a pink tint to their fingers for up to a day after cutting beets. If this is a concern, you can wear gloves to protect your hands and an apron to protect your clothes.

Roasted Beets 'n' Sweets

Chapter 10

Pleasing Pastas, Rice, and Beans

Whether it's a main dish or a side dish, the slow cooker turns pastas, rice, and beans into easy cooking. In some of the pasta recipes in this chapter, the noodles cook directly in the slow cooker, while others call for cooking the pasta on the stove according to the package directions. With pastas that are traditionally baked, like lasagna and macaroni and cheese, the noodles can cook in the slow cooker. Sauce-based dishes are best served over freshly cooked pasta to avoid mushy noodles.

Using slow cooker liners or lining the slow cooker with aluminum foil is particularly useful for pastas and rice to prevent sticking.

Classic Italian Lasagna

Layers of saucy sausage and ground beef, a melty combination of four different cheeses, lasagna pasta, and Italian spices make this a classic dish, with the ease of the slow cooker.

Yield	8 slices
Serving Size	1 slice
Prep Time	20 minutes
Cook Time	4 to 6 hours

1 lb. (450g) ground beef

1 lb. (450g) ground pork sausage

1 medium yellow onion, diced

4 cloves garlic, minced

1 tsp. salt

1 tsp. dried basil

1 tsp. dried oregano

4 cups marinara sauce

16 oz. (450g) ricotta cheese

1 large egg

1 TB. dried parsley

10 oven-ready lasagna pasta sheets

3 cups shredded mozzarella cheese

6 slices provolone cheese

½ cup shredded Parmesan cheese

1. In a large skillet over medium-high heat, cook ground beef, ground sausage, and yellow onion, stirring occasionally, for 7 to 10 minutes or until meat is browned. Drain any excess fat from the pan.

2. Stir in garlic, salt, basil, oregano, and marinara sauce.

3. Scoop a spoonful of sauce mixture into the bottom of a 6- to 8-quart (5.5- to 7.5-liter) oval slow cooker.

4. In a small bowl, whisk together ricotta cheese, egg, and parsley.

5. Place 2 lasagna pasta sheets parallel in the bottom of the slow cooker. Break another pasta sheet in half and place on the ends of the oval. (Pasta sheets will expand as they cook.) Top with ⅓ ricotta mixture, followed by ¼ sauce mixture, and 1 cup mozzarella cheese.

6. Next, layer 3 pasta sheets as before, topped by ⅓ ricotta mixture, ¼ sauce mixture, and provolone cheese.

7. Finally, layer 3 pasta sheets as before, topped by remaining ricotta cheese, ¼ sauce mixture, and 1 cup mozzarella.

8. Top with remaining 3 pasta sheets and remaining sauce mixture. Sprinkle with remaining 1 cup mozzarella and Parmesan cheese.

9. Cover and cook on low for 4 to 6 hours.

10. Cut into 8 slices, and serve hot.

Variation: For **Spinach Lasagna,** add 10 ounces (285 grams) frozen spinach, thawed and thoroughly drained, evenly divided on top of each ricotta layer.

A homemade cheese-filled white sauce is the basis for this layered vegetable lasagna starring artichoke, spinach, and sun-dried tomatoes.

Yield	8 slices
Serving Size	1 slice
Prep Time	20 minutes
Cook Time	4 to 6 hours

½ cup butter

1 medium yellow onion, diced

2 cloves garlic, minced

½ cup all-purpose flour

1 tsp. salt

2 cups vegetable broth

1½ cups milk

3 cups shredded mozzarella cheese

1 tsp. dried basil

1 tsp. dried oregano

½ tsp. black pepper

10 oz. (285g) frozen spinach, thawed and drained well

2 cups chopped artichoke hearts

½ cups sun-dried tomatoes, roughly chopped

10 oven-ready lasagna pasta sheets

16 oz. (450g) ricotta cheese

1 cup grated Parmesan cheese

1. In a large saucepan over low heat, melt butter.

2. Increase heat to medium-high, stir in yellow onion, and sauté, stirring occasionally, for about 4 minutes.

3. Add garlic and cook for about 1 more minute.

4. Stir in all-purpose flour and salt to form a thick paste.

5. Slowly stir in vegetable broth and milk, bring to a boil, and simmer for 90 seconds to allow sauce to thicken. Remove from heat.

6. Stir in 2 cups mozzarella cheese, basil, oregano, and black pepper until cheese is melted and creamy.

7. In a medium bowl, combine drained spinach, artichoke hearts, and sun-dried tomatoes.

8. Scoop a spoonful of sauce into the bottom of a 6- to 8-quart (5.5- to 7.5-liter) oval slow cooker. Place 2 lasagna pasta sheets parallel in the bottom of the slow cooker. Break another pasta sheet in half and place on the ends of the oval. (Pasta sheets will expand as they cook.) Top with ⅓ ricotta, followed by ⅓ spinach mixture and ¼ cheese sauce. Repeat two more times to create three layers. Top with remaining 3 pasta sheets, and sprinkle mozzarella cheese and Parmesan cheese over top.

9. Cover and cook on low for 4 to 6 hours.

10. Slice into 8 slices and serve hot.

White Vegetable Lasagna

Tri-Tip Beef Stroganoff

A creamy, dark mushroom sauce coats tender beef tri-tip in this comfort classic pasta dish served over egg noodles. The meat is the highlight of the pasta, practically falling apart with slow cooked tenderness.

Yield	12 cups
Serving Size	2 cups
Prep Time	5 minutes
Cook Time	8 hours

2 lb. (1kg) tri-tip beef roast

1 tsp. salt

½ tsp. black pepper

1 TB. cornstarch

2 cups beef broth

1 medium yellow onion, diced

8 oz. (225g) mushrooms, sliced

¾ cup sour cream

¼ cup sliced green onions, green parts only

1 lb. (450g) egg noodles

1. Place tri-tip roast in the bottom of a 6- to 8-quart (5.5- to 7.5-liter) slow cooker. Season with salt and black pepper.

2. In a small bowl, combine cornstarch with 1 tablespoon beef broth. Stir cornstarch mixture into remaining beef broth, and pour around tri-tip.

3. Top roast with yellow onion and mushrooms.

4. Cover and cook on low for 8 hours.

5. Remove roast from the slow cooker and cut into bite-size chunks. Return meat to the slow cooker, stir in sour cream, and top with green onions.

6. Cook egg noodles according to the package directions.

7. Serve meat sauce hot on top of cooked egg noodles.

Keeping the mushrooms on top of the meat and out of the liquid prevents them from getting soggy during the slow cooking process.

Large and flavorful meatballs are slowly cooked in a homemade spaghetti sauce. Making this classic dish from scratch is simplified using the low and slow method a slow cooker offers.

Yield	12 cups
Serving Size	2 cups
Prep Time	15 minutes
Cook Time	3 or 4 hours

2 (15-oz.; 420g) cans diced tomatoes, drained

2 TB. tomato paste

½ medium yellow onion, diced

4 cloves garlic, minced

1½ tsp. salt

1 tsp. sugar

2 tsp. dried basil

½ tsp. black pepper

1 lb. (450g) lean ground beef

⅓ cup dried breadcrumbs

¼ cup grated Parmesan cheese

½ tsp. crushed red pepper flakes

3 TB. milk

2 TB. Worcestershire sauce

1 lb. (450g) uncooked spaghetti

1. In a food processor fitted with an S blade or in a blender, purée tomatoes, tomato paste, yellow onion, 2 cloves garlic, 1 teaspoon salt, sugar, 1 teaspoon basil, and black pepper until smooth. Pour tomato sauce into a 6- to 8-quart (5.5- to 7.5-liter) slow cooker.

2. In a medium bowl, combine ground beef, breadcrumbs, Parmesan cheese, remaining 2 cloves garlic, remaining 1 teaspoon basil, remaining ½ teaspoon salt, crushed red pepper flakes, milk, and Worcestershire sauce. Using your hands, knead mixture until well mixed and form into 12 meatballs. Place meatballs into sauce in the slow cooker.

3. Cover and cook on high for 3 or 4 hours.

4. Cook spaghetti according to the package directions.

5. Serve spaghetti hot, topped with sauce and meatballs.

Making **Homemade Spaghetti Sauce** is simple in the slow cooker, and it's easy to prepare a large batch. In a 6- to 8-quart (5.5- to 7.5-liter) slow cooker, combine 10 (14-ounce; 400-gram) cans diced tomatoes or 10 pounds (4.5 kilograms) fresh roma tomatoes, peeled and cored; ¼ cup olive oil; 3 medium yellow onions, diced; 10 cloves garlic, minced; 1 tablespoon salt; 3 teaspoons sugar; 3 tablespoons dried basil; and 1 teaspoon black pepper. Cover and cook on low for 4 to 6 hours. Transfer in batches to a food processor fitted with an S blade or a blender, and purée until smooth, or use an immersion blender. Divide sauce and freeze in resealable plastic freezer bags.

Spaghetti and Meatballs

Secret Ingredient Macaroni and Cheese

A creamy cheddar cheese sauce embraces elbow macaroni pasta in this slow cooked home-style favorite. The not-so-secret ingredient, cayenne hot sauce, enhances the flavor of the cheddar without adding much, if any, heat.

Yield	8 cups
Serving Size	1 cup
Prep Time	5 minutes
Cook Time	2 or 3 hours

½ cup butter, melted

½ cup all-purpose flour

1 tsp. salt

1½ tsp. ground mustard

1½ tsp. onion powder

½ tsp. white pepper

5 cups milk

2 TB. cayenne hot sauce

1 lb. (450g) uncooked elbow macaroni pasta

2½ cups shredded sharp cheddar cheese

1. In a large bowl, whisk together butter, all-purpose flour, salt, ground mustard, onion powder, and white pepper to form paste. Slowly whisk in milk, and stir in cayenne hot sauce.

2. In a 6- to 8-quart (5.5- to 7.5-liter) slow cooker, place elbow macaroni and sharp cheddar cheese. Pour in milk mixture and stir to combine. Pat down macaroni so it's covered in sauce.

3. Cover and cook on low for 2 or 3 hours or until milk is absorbed and pasta is cooked.

Variation: For **Bacon Mac and Cheese,** add 1 pound (450 grams) bacon, cooked and crumbled, just before serving.

It's all too easy to overcook pasta in the slow cooker, so be sure to check the macaroni at the lowest end of the cook time range to see if it's done.

Cayenne hot sauce (also called cayenne pepper hot sauce) is most often used for buffalo wings. You can find it in many grocery stores in the condiment section.

In this versatile comfort food recipe, filled pastas are smothered between layers of cheese and finished off with classic tomato marinara sauce.

Yield	2 cups
Serving Size	1 cup
Prep Time	5 minutes
Cook Time	5 to 6 hours

50 oz. (1.5kg) frozen ravioli

3 cups shredded mozzarella cheese

1 cup shredded Parmesan cheese

3 cups marinara sauce

1. In a 6- to 8-quart (5.5- to 7.5-liter) slow cooker, place ⅓ ravioli. Top with 1 cup mozzarella cheese and ⅓ cup Parmesan cheese.

2. Create two more layers in the same fashion, each with ⅓ ravioli topped with 1 cup mozzarella and ⅓ cup Parmesan.

3. Pour marinara sauce over pasta.

4. Cover and cook on low for 5 or 6 hours or until cheeses are melted and ravioli are heated through.

5. Serve hot.

Variation: Add a layer of sautéed onion and garlic on top of the pasta. In a large skillet over medium-high heat, heat 1 tablespoon olive oil. Add 1 medium yellow onion, diced, and 4 cloves minced garlic, and sauté for 5 to 7 minutes.

Many flavors of ravioli are available today. Simple meat-and-cheese-filled ravioli are the most common, but you also can find more gourmet flavors like mushroom, spinach, butternut squash, or even lobster. Any of these varieties can be used in this recipe. If you're using fresh, not frozen, ravioli in this recipe, reduce the cook time by 1 or 2 hours.

Cheesy Ravioli Casserole

Brown Rice and Black Bean Casserole

Hearty brown rice is mixed with black beans, zucchini, carrots, and mushrooms in this healthy dish. Try it as a main course or a side.

Yield	6 cups
Serving Size	1 cup
Prep Time	10 minutes
Cook Time	3 or 4 hours

1½ cups long-grain brown rice

3 cups vegetable broth

1 TB. olive oil

1 tsp. ground cumin

3 cloves garlic, minced

1 medium yellow onion, diced

1 (15-oz.; 420g) can black beans, drained and rinsed

1 (4-oz.; 110g) can diced green chiles, with liquid

1 medium zucchini, stem removed and diced

3 large carrots, peeled and shredded

8 oz. (225g) button mushrooms, sliced

2 cups shredded mozzarella cheese

1. In a 6- to 8-quart (5.5- to 7.5-liter) slow cooker, place long-grain brown rice. Pour in vegetable broth and olive oil, and season with cumin and garlic.

2. Top rice mixture with yellow onion, black beans, green chiles, zucchini, and carrots. Layer button mushrooms on top.

3. Cover and cook on high for 3 or 4 hours or until rice is cooked and liquids are absorbed.

4. Top hot rice with mozzarella cheese and let melt.

5. Serve hot.

Variation: Cut 2 pounds (1 kilogram) boneless-skinless chicken breasts into bite-size pieces, and layer on top of rice. Check chicken for doneness before serving.

The traditional method cooking of brown rice takes 40 to 60 minutes, whereas it only takes about 15 minutes to cook white rice. The hearty texture of brown rice makes it stand up really well in slow cooking.

This traditionally time-intensive creamy rice dish is simple in the slow cooker. Arborio rice soaks in chicken broth to create a creamy starch sauce that's served topped with freshly sautéed mushrooms.

Yield	6 cups
Serving Size	1 cup
Prep Time	10 minutes
Cook Time	2 or 3 hours

6 cups chicken broth

1½ cups arborio rice

½ medium yellow onion, diced

1 tsp. salt

½ tsp. black pepper

4 TB. butter

⅓ cup grated Parmesan cheese

2 TB. olive oil

16 oz. (450g) mushrooms, sliced

1. In a 4- to 6-quart (4- to 5.5-liter) slow cooker, combine chicken broth, arborio rice, yellow onion, salt, and black pepper.

2. Cover and cook on high for 2 or 3 hours or until rice has absorbed broth.

3. Remove rice from the slow cooker, and stir in butter and Parmesan cheese until melted.

4. In a large skillet over high heat, heat olive oil. Add mushrooms, and cook, stirring occasionally, for 3 to 5 minutes.

5. Top rice with cooked mushrooms and serve hot.

The mushrooms are added at the end of this recipe to keep them fresh and not soggy. Until they're added, this recipe is a nice, easily adaptable base recipe for risotto. You can also add various vegetables to the risotto and steam them on top of the rice. Try asparagus, broccoli, or fennel, for example.

Creamy Mushroom Risotto

Un-Fried Rice

In this easy, slow cooked dish, you get all the sesame and soy flavors of restaurant-style fried rice without the frying. Carrots and peas add color and more flavor in this tasty side.

Yield	6 cups
Serving Size	1 cup
Prep Time	10 minutes
Cook Time	2 or 3 hours

2 cups long-grain white rice

4 cups water

2 TB. olive oil

2 TB. soy sauce

1 TB. toasted sesame oil

1 medium yellow onion, diced

4 medium carrots, peeled and diced

½ cup frozen peas, thawed

1. In a 6- to 8-quart (5.5- to 7.5-liter) slow cooker, place long-grain white rice. Add water, olive oil, soy sauce, and sesame oil.

2. Sprinkle yellow onion, carrots, and peas on top of rice mixture.

3. Cover and cook on high for 2 or 3 hours or until rice is cooked through and liquids have been absorbed.

4. Serve hot.

Variation: You can crack 1 or 2 eggs on top of the cooked rice and cook on high for 1 more hour or until the egg is cooked through. Stir and serve.

Sesame oil is a vegetable oil derived from sesame seeds. Toasted sesame oil comes from toasted sesame seeds and has a strong, nutty flavor. You can find both regular and toasted versions in most well-stocked grocery stores in the international section near items like soy sauce.

Tomatoes and chili powder give this rice dish its bright red color. Onions, bell peppers, green chiles, and garlic give it a flavor reminiscent of salsa, making it a perfect partner with other Mexican dishes.

Yield	6 cups
Serving Size	1 cup
Prep Time	5 minutes
Cook Time	2 or 3 hours

1 cup long-grain white rice

2 cups chicken broth

1 tsp. salt

1 tsp. chili powder

1 medium yellow onion, diced

1 large green bell pepper, ribs and seeds removed, and diced

1 (4-oz.; 110g) can diced green chiles, with liquid

1 (15-oz.; 420g) can diced tomatoes, with juice

3 cloves garlic, minced

1. In a 4- to 6-quart (4- to 5.5-liter) slow cooker, place long-grain white rice.

2. Pour in chicken broth, season with salt and chili powder, and stir to combine.

3. Layer in yellow onion, green bell pepper, and green chiles with liquid, and top with tomatoes and juice and garlic.

4. Cover and cook on high for 2 or 3 hours or until rice is cooked through.

5. Stir to combine, and serve hot.

This dish doesn't come from Spain—it's actually a dish native to the southwestern United States, where it's usually served as an accompaniment to Mexican cuisine. The name references the language spoken in Mexico rather than the country of origin. Similar dishes are served in Mexico under various names, but most commonly it's just referred to as rice.

Spanish Rice

Boston Baked Beans

Sweet and salty navy beans are cooked low and slow in this classic bean dish. Molasses and brown sugar provide the signature sweetness that makes this recipe a family favorite.

Yield	8 cups
Serving Size	1 cup
Prep Time	10 minutes, plus 8 hours soak time
Cook Time	8 to 10 hours

3 cups dry navy beans

12 cups water

1 medium yellow onion, diced

1 large red bell pepper, ribs and stems removed, and diced

¼ cup molasses

1 cup brown sugar, firmly packed

2½ cups ketchup

2 TB. Worcestershire sauce

1 tsp. salt

1 tsp. garlic powder

1 tsp. chili powder

½ tsp. ground mustard

½ tsp. black pepper

1. In a large bowl, cover navy beans with water, and set aside to soak for 8 hours or overnight.

2. Drain beans and transfer to a 6- to 8-quart (5.5- to 7.5-liter) slow cooker.

3. Stir in yellow onion, red bell pepper, molasses, brown sugar, ketchup, Worcestershire sauce, salt, garlic powder, chili powder, ground mustard, and black pepper.

4. Cover and cook on low for 8 to 10 hours.

Variation: For a smoky pork flavor, add 1 pound (450 grams) bacon, cooked and crumbled, just before serving.

There's a debate in the culinary world about whether soaking beans is even necessary. Soaking shortens the beans' cook time, but it might not really do much more than that. Navy beans are quite hard and benefit from the shortened cook time that comes from soaking. Without soaking, navy beans may take 14 to 16 hours or more to cook in the slow cooker.

When working with dried beans, before soaking them or adding them to your recipe, be sure to pick through them. Sort through the beans, and pick out any stones, debris, or damaged beans you find.

Refried beans are a staple side in Mexican cuisine. Seasoned with onion, garlic, and jalapeño, and given a richness from the butter, these beans are tasty, flavorful dish.

Yield	6 cups
Serving Size	½ cup
Prep Time	10 minutes
Cook Time	8 to 10 hours

3 cups dry pinto beans

1 tsp. salt

1 medium yellow onion, diced

4 cloves garlic, minced

1 jalapeño, stem removed, and minced

9 cups water

½ cup butter

1. Pick through pinto beans, and remove any stones or shriveled beans. Place beans in a 6- to 8-quart (5.5- to 7.5-liter) slow cooker.

2. Stir in salt, yellow onion, garlic, and jalapeño, and pour in water.

3. Cover and cook on low for 8 to 10 hours.

4. Transfer beans to a colander to drain.

5. In a food processor fitted with an S blade, purée beans, or mash by hand with a potato masher.

6. Stir in butter until completely melted.

7. Serve hot.

Variation: For a fat-free version, you can omit the butter.

Traditionally, refried beans are made by cooking the beans and then frying them in lard with spices. If you like, you can use the same amount of lard in place of butter for a more authentic flavor.

Mexican Refried Beans

White Beans and Pancetta

White beans and salty pancetta cook together in this subtle yet flavorful bean dish. This side pairs well with Italian meals.

Yield	6 cups
Serving Size	1 cup
Prep Time	10 minutes
Cook Time	8 to 10 hours

2 cups dry Great Northern beans

8 cups chicken broth

½ tsp. salt

4 oz. (110g) diced pancetta

1 medium yellow onion, diced

4 cloves garlic, minced

1. In a 6- to 8-quart (5.5- to 7.5-liter) slow cooker, place Great Northern beans. Pour in chicken broth, and stir in salt.

2. In a large skillet over medium-high heat, cook pancetta and yellow onion, stirring occasionally, for 5 to 7 minutes. Add garlic during the last minute of cooking.

3. Transfer pancetta and onion to the slow cooker.

4. Cover and cook.

Variation: For an earthy flavor, stir in 2 tablespoons dried rosemary with the garlic.

Pancetta is an Italian bacon. Although it's cut from the same part of the pig, the difference comes in the curing: bacon is smoked, whereas pancetta is not. The two can be used interchangeably in recipes; using bacon will add a smoky element to a dish.

Chapter 11

Bountiful Breads

You can create delightful breads, rolls, and more in your slow cooker—no rising time required! A parchment paper liner is used in most of the recipes so you can quickly and easily remove the finished bread so it doesn't continue to cook from the heat of the stoneware insert. And because slow cooker breads can sometimes burn on the side opposite the control panels, where the stoneware gets the hottest, you might want to construct a protective heat barrier. Fold a 12-inch (30-centimeter) piece of aluminum foil lengthwise in half three times, and place it in the insert before preparing the recipe. Or use traditional bread pans. If it fits in your cooker, you can use it. The cook time will be a bit longer, but you'll avoid any burned edges or uncooked centers.

The moisture of the slow cooker creates an easy and versatile peasant-style loaf bread with a chewy crust and a soft interior. Shape it however you'd like, from a baguette to a round loaf.

Yield	1 loaf
Serving Size	1 slice
Prep Time	5 minutes
Cook Time	2 or 3 hours

1½ tsp. instant dry yeast

1½ tsp. salt

1 cup lukewarm water

2 to 2½ cups all-purpose flour

1. In a large bowl, and using an electric mixer on medium speed, combine instant dry yeast, salt, lukewarm water, and 2 cups all-purpose flour. Continue to knead on medium until mixture forms a dough ball, adding more flour as necessary to prevent dough from sticking to the sides of the bowl.

2. Remove dough from the bowl and use your hands to shape dough into the desired loaf shape. Place in a 6- to 8-quart (5.5- to 7.5-liter) slow cooker.

3. Cover and cook on high for 2 or 3 hours or until loaf sounds hollow when thumped.

4. Immediately remove bread from the slow cooker and transfer to a wire rack to cool.

Variation: For **Crusty Herb Bread,** knead dried herbs into the dough in step 1. Try 1 teaspoon dried rosemary, basil, or your choice herb, or a combination equaling 1 teaspoon. For **Garlic Loaf,** add 2 cloves garlic, minced.

Slicing the tops of bread loaves is traditionally done to prevent the loaves from cracking during baking. The slow cooking method doesn't require slicing, but you can still do this for aesthetic purposes. Use a sharp knife to slash a few parallel ¼-inch-deep (.5-centimeter-deep) slices into the top of the dough before baking.

Crusty Loaf Bread

Dinner Rolls

These soft, pull-apart dinner rolls are perfect for buttering and serving alongside all kinds of dinners.

Yield	12 rolls
Serving Size	1 roll
Prep Time	5 minutes
Cook Time	2 or 3 hours

1 cup warm milk

2 TB. instant dry yeast

1 TB. sugar

1 tsp. salt

3 TB. butter, softened

1 large egg

2½ to 3 cups all-purpose flour

1. Line a 6- to 8-quart (5.5- to 7.5-liter) slow cooker with parchment paper.

2. In a large bowl, combine warm milk, instant dry yeast, sugar, and salt.

3. Using an electric mixer fitted with a dough hook on medium speed, mix in butter, egg, and 2½ cups all-purpose flour until dough pulls away from the sides of the bowl. Add remaining ½ cup flour as necessary to prevent sticking.

4. Divide dough into 12 pieces, roll into balls, and place in the bottom of the prepared slow cooker so they're touching.

5. Cover and cook on high for 2 or 3 hours.

6. Remove rolls from the slow cooker and serve warm, or cool on a wire rack.

Variation: Brush the tops of the cooked rolls with 2 tablespoons melted butter when you remove them from the slow cooker for shiny, buttery rolls.

The slow heating process of the slow cooker builds the rising time into the cooking time. By the time the slow cooker reaches maximum temperature (200°F; 90°C), the yeast has had time to work and the dough has begun to rise and cook.

Fluffy focaccia is sprinkled with sea salt and rosemary in this olive oil–glazed Italian bread. The slow cooker yields a crispy bottom crust and a steamed top that's perfectly delicious.

Yield	10 pieces
Serving Size	1 piece
Prep Time	5 minutes
Cook Time	2 hours

1 cup warm water

1½ tsp. salt

1½ tsp. instant dry yeast

1½ tsp. sugar

2 TB. olive oil

2 to 2½ cups all-purpose flour

1 tsp. dried rosemary

¼ tsp. sea salt

1. In a large bowl, combine warm water, salt, instant dry yeast, sugar, 1 tablespoon olive oil, and 2 cups all-purpose flour.

2. Using an electric mixer fitted with a dough hook on medium speed, knead until dough pulls away from the sides of the bowl and forms a large dough ball. Add remaining ½ cup flour as necessary to prevent sticking.

3. Turn out dough onto a lightly floured surface, and roll to ½ inch (1.25 centimeters) thick.

4. Use your hands to stretch dough to fit the shape of the bottom of a 6- to 8-quart (5.5- to 7.5-liter) slow cooker, and place dough in the slow cooker.

5. Drizzle remaining 1 tablespoon olive oil over dough, and sprinkle with rosemary and sea salt. Use your fingertips to create indentations all over dough.

6. Cover and cook on high for 2 hours.

7. Remove focaccia from the slow cooker, and cool on a wire rack.

Variation: For **Olive Focaccia Bread,** add ½ cup sliced olives to the top of the dough in step 5 with the olive oil. When creating indentations in the dough, gently press the olives into the loaf.

Creating indentations in the dough gives the finished focaccia its typical dotted look and makes small wells for the olive oil to puddle in, keeping the bread moist.

Rosemary Focaccia Bread with Sea Salt

Rye Bread

Caraway plays the starring role in this delicious light rye. You can create a dark rye version of this staple Eastern European bread just by adding a few simple ingredients.

Yield	1 loaf
Serving Size	1 slice
Prep Time	5 minutes
Cook Time	2 or 3 hours

1½ tsp. instant dry yeast

2 cups water

2 tsp. caraway seeds

1 tsp. salt

1 cup rye flour

1 to 1½ cups all-purpose flour

1. In a large bowl, combine instant dry yeast, water, caraway seeds, salt, rye flour, and 1 cup all-purpose flour.

2. Using an electric mixer fitted with a dough hook on medium speed, knead dough until it pulls away from the sides of the bowl and forms a large dough ball. Add remaining ½ cup flour as necessary to prevent sticking.

3. Shape dough into a ball and place in the bottom of a 6- to 8-quart (5.5- to 7.5-liter) slow cooker.

4. Cover and cook on high for 2 or 3 hours.

5. Remove loaf from the slow cooker, and cool on a wire rack.

Variation: For **Dark Rye Bread,** add 3 tablespoons dark brown sugar, 2 tablespoons molasses, and 1 tablespoon cocoa powder with the flours. You probably won't need as much all-purpose flour, and likely won't use the full remaining ½ cup in step 2.

In the United States, rye bread is often used for sandwiches. (Nothing beats a tuna on rye, and Reuben sandwiches wouldn't be the same without the rye.) Don't limit your rye to just sandwiches, though. Make it into toast, or just enjoy the distinct flavors of caraway and rye plain as a side.

This sweet, slow cooked cornbread is incredibly moist. Sweetened with a little sugar and loaded with cornmeal, the result is a bright yellow cornbread that's perfect alongside soups, stews, and many other dishes.

Yield	10 slices
Serving Size	1 slice
Prep Time	5 minutes
Cook Time	2 or 3 hours

½ cup butter, melted

⅔ cup sugar

2 large eggs

1 cup buttermilk

1 cup yellow cornmeal

1 cup all-purpose flour

½ tsp. baking soda

½ tsp. salt

1. Line a 6- to 8-quart (5.5- to 7.5-liter) slow cooker with an aluminum foil barrier and parchment paper.

2. In a large bowl, whisk together melted butter, sugar, eggs, and buttermilk until well combined.

3. Stir in yellow cornmeal, all-purpose flour, baking soda, and salt until smooth.

4. Pour batter into the prepared slow cooker.

5. Cover and cook on high for 2 or 3 hours or until center of cornbread is set.

6. Remove cornbread from the slow cooker and cool on a wire rack.

Variation: For a chunky-style cornbread, add 1 cup frozen corn kernels, thawed and drained, to the dough in step 3.

Cornbread made traditionally in the southern United States is made without any sugar, while most nonsoutherners are accustomed to the sweetened version.

Cornbread

Banana Bread

Over-ripe bananas add a strong banana flavor to this sweet, moist bread, while walnuts bring a pleasant crunch.

Yield	2 mini loaves or 1 regular loaf
Serving Size	1 slice
Prep Time	5 minutes
Cook Time	2 or 3 hours

¼ cup butter, melted

½ cup sugar

1 large egg

½ tsp. vanilla extract

¾ cup all-purpose flour

½ tsp. baking soda

¼ tsp. salt

¼ cup sour cream

¼ cup chopped walnuts

1 medium banana, peeled and mashed

1. Lightly coat 2 mini (4½×2¾×1¼-inch; 11.5×7×3-centimeter) loaf pans or 1 regular (9×5×3-inch; 23×12.5×7.5-centimeter) loaf pan with nonstick cooking spray. Be sure the pan(s) fit into a 6- to 8-quart (5.5- to 7.5-liter) slow cooker.

2. In a large bowl, combine melted butter, sugar, egg, and vanilla extract until egg is well incorporated.

3. Stir in all-purpose flour, baking soda, and salt until smooth.

4. Fold in sour cream, walnuts, and banana.

5. Pour batter into the prepared pan(s), and set the pan(s) in the slow cooker.

6. Cover and cook on high for 2 or 3 hours or until center of bread is set.

7. Remove the pans from the slow cooker and cool on a wire rack before removing bread from the pans.

Variation: You can easily double this recipe and cook the bread in a 6- to 8-quart (5.5- to 7.5-liter) slow cooker lined with parchment paper.

Bananas don't "go bad" as much as they change stages of ripeness. Bananas start out green and turn yellow as they ripen. Black spots start to appear after a few days, signifying a change in the bananas' ripeness—and sweetness. Spotted bananas are sweeter. Bananas that have completely black skins have an intense flavor and are best for use in breads, puddings, and pies.

This favorite quick bread is flavored with pumpkin and spiced with the classic combination of cinnamon, nutmeg, cloves, and just a pinch of ginger.

Yield	2 mini loaves or 1 regular loaf
Serving Size	1 slice
Prep Time	5 minutes
Cook Time	2 or 3 hours

1 cup pumpkin purée

2 large eggs

½ cup applesauce

⅓ cup water

1½ cups sugar

1¾ cups all-purpose flour

1 tsp. baking soda

¾ tsp. salt

½ tsp. ground cinnamon

½ tsp. ground nutmeg

¼ tsp. ground cloves

⅛ tsp. ground ginger

1. Lightly coat 2 mini (4½×2¾×1¼-inch; 11.5×7×3-centimeter) loaf pans or 1 regular (9×5×3-inch; 23×12.5×7.5-centimeter) loaf pan with nonstick cooking spray. Be sure the pan(s) fit into a 6- to 8-quart (5.5- to 7.5-liter) slow cooker.

2. In a large bowl, combine pumpkin purée, eggs, applesauce, water, sugar, all-purpose flour, baking soda, salt, cinnamon, nutmeg, cloves, and ginger until smooth.

3. Pour batter into the prepared loaf pan(s), and set the pan(s) in the slow cooker.

4. Cover and cook on high for 2 or 3 hours or until center of bread is set.

5. Remove the pans from the slow cooker and cool on a wire rack before removing bread from the pans.

Variation: For **Chocolate-Chip Pumpkin Bread,** add ½ cup mini chocolate chips to the batter.

If you don't have a pan that can fit into your slow cooker, you can cook this bread in the stoneware insert lined with an aluminum foil barrier and parchment paper. Doubling the recipe provides enough batter to yield a nice loaf of bread when cooked in a 6- to 8-quart (5.5- to 7.5-liter) slow cooker.

Pumpkin Bread

Chapter 12

Slow Cooker Sweets

Perhaps the most pleasant surprise of the slow cooker is its ability to produce some amazing desserts with absolute ease. What's more, the cook times are generally short, so you can get your dessert going first and have it hot and ready when dinner is over. This is particularly useful when hosting guests or dinner parties, and frees you to enjoy your company instead of being stuck in the kitchen cooking.

Apple Dumplings

Soft and warm sugar-and-spice apples are wrapped in a sweet pastry dough and drizzled with a cinnamon buttermilk syrup for an updated version of this old-fashioned favorite.

Yield	4 dumplings
Serving Size	1 dumpling
Prep Time	20 minutes
Cook Time	3 or 4 hours

2 cups all-purpose flour

¾ cup confectioners' sugar

1 TB. baking powder

1 tsp. salt

1¼ cups butter

½ cup milk

¼ cup brown sugar, firmly packed

1½ tsp. ground cinnamon

½ tsp. ground nutmeg

6 medium Granny Smith apples, peeled and cored

1 cup sugar

1 cup buttermilk

1 TB. vanilla extract

½ tsp. baking soda

> Don't substitute puff pastry for the dough made in this recipe. Puff pastry requires a blast of heat in order to puff.

1. In a large bowl, combine all-purpose flour, confectioners' sugar, baking powder, and salt.

2. Using a pastry cutter or 2 butter knives, cut ½ cup butter into flour mixture until it resembles coarse meal.

3. Pour in milk, and using your hands, knead mixture into ball of dough.

4. Turn out dough onto a lightly floured flat surface, and using a rolling pin, roll dough into a ¼-inch-thick (.5-centimeter-thick) square. Cut into 4 squares.

5. In a small bowl, combine ¼ cup butter, brown sugar, 1 teaspoon cinnamon, and nutmeg.

6. Place 1 apple on each dough square. Divide brown sugar mixture among apples, filling the hollowed-out core.

7. Gently pull dough up and around apple, wrapping entire apple in dough and pinching any seams together. Place wrapped apples in a 6- to 8-quart (5.5- to 7.5-liter) slow cooker.

8. Cover and cook on high for 3 or 4 hours.

9. In a large saucepan over medium heat, melt remaining ½ cup butter. Stir in sugar, buttermilk, vanilla extract, and remaining ½ teaspoon cinnamon. Increase heat to high, bring to a boil, and boil for 90 seconds. Remove from heat and stir in baking soda until foam dissipates.

10. Serve apple dumplings hot with syrup poured over top.

Cinnamon and sugar–coated apples are cooked to a delicate caramelized state and topped with a brown sugar and oat crumble.

Yield	8 cups
Serving Size	1 cup
Prep Time	15 minutes
Cook Time	3 or 4 hours

10 medium apples, peeled, cored, and sliced

1 cup sugar

1 tsp. cornstarch

1 tsp. ground cinnamon

1 cup quick oats

1 cup all-purpose flour

1 cup brown sugar, firmly packed

¼ tsp. baking powder

¼ tsp. baking soda

½ cup butter

1. In a 6- to 8-quart (5.5- to 7.5-liter) slow cooker, combine apples with sugar, cornstarch, and cinnamon.

2. In a medium bowl, combine quick oats, all-purpose flour, brown sugar, baking powder, and baking soda.

3. Using a pastry cutter or 2 butter knives, cut butter into flour mixture until it resembles a coarse meal.

4. Sprinkle oat mixture over apples in the slow cooker.

5. Cover and cook on high for 3 or 4 hours or until apples are tender.

6. Serve hot.

Variation: For an **Apple-Blueberry Crumble,** replace 2 apples with 2 cups fresh or frozen blueberries (thawed, if frozen).

Thousands of varieties of apples are grown all over the world. Some of the most commonly available are Gala, Golden Delicious, Granny Smith, Honeycrisp, McIntosh, and Red Delicious. Each has its own distinct characteristics. Gala, Golden Delicious, Granny Smith, and Honeycrisp, each with a different balance of sweet and tart, are great for all-around cooking. McIntoshes break down more easily and are great for applesauce, but in an apple dessert, you might want apples that hold their shape better. It's best not to bake with Red Delicious apples. They're better eaten out of hand.

Apple Crumble

Peach Cobbler

Peaches sweetened with sugar and brightened with lemon serve as the base in this tasty cobbler. A sweet biscuit dough is heaped on top to provide the ultimate cobbler top.

Yield	8 cups
Serving Size	1 cup
Prep Time	30 minutes
Cook Time	3 or 4 hours

8 medium fresh peaches, pitted, peeled, and sliced

⅓ cup sugar

Zest of 1 medium lemon

Juice of 1 medium lemon

2 tsp. cornstarch

½ tsp. vanilla extract

2 cups all-purpose flour

1 tsp. salt

1 TB. baking powder

¾ cup confectioners' sugar

½ cup butter

1 cup half-and-half

1. In a 6- to 8-quart (5.5- to 7.5-liter) slow cooker, place peaches. Add sugar, lemon zest, lemon juice, cornstarch, and vanilla extract, and toss to combine.

2. In a large bowl, combine all-purpose flour, salt, baking powder, and confectioners' sugar. Using a pastry cutter or 2 butter knives, cut butter into flour mixture until it resembles cornmeal.

3. Slowly stir in half-and-half to form thick batter. Spoon batter over peaches in large heaps.

4. Cover and cook on high for 3 or 4 hours or until dough is cooked through.

5. Serve hot.

Variation: If peaches are not in season, you can use 4 (15-ounce; 420-gram) cans peaches in water (not syrup), drained.

This recipe is so easy to customize. For a **Berry Cobbler,** use a mixture of 3 cups berries instead of peaches. For **Apple Cobbler,** use 8 medium apples, peeled, cored, and sliced.

Sweet, juicy pears are cooked to tender perfection in a tart, acidic, and sweet vanilla-orange syrup. Cinnamon adds a warm and inviting flavor to this fantastic fruit dessert.

Yield	6 pears
Serving Size	1 pear
Prep Time	10 minutes
Cook Time	2 hours

6 medium pears, peeled

1½ cups orange juice

½ cup brown sugar, firmly packed

¼ cup sugar

1 TB. vanilla extract

1 tsp. ground cinnamon

1. Core pears from the bottom, leaving stem intact. Place cored pears on their sides in a 6- to 8-quart (5.5- to 7.5-liter) slow cooker.

2. In a medium bowl, whisk together orange juice, brown sugar, sugar, vanilla extract, and cinnamon. Pour syrup over pears.

3. Cover and cook on high for 1 hour.

4. Flip over pears, cover, and cook on high for 1 more hour or until pears are soft.

5. Serve hot, drizzled with juices.

You could stand the pears upright in the slow cooker and baste them with the syrup later, but turning them on their sides allows them to soak in the flavors of the syrup. Flipping them halfway through the cook time ensures you get fully poached pears.

Vanilla-Orange Poached Pears

Salted Caramel Rice Pudding

Creamy rice pudding is swirled with a homemade salted caramel sauce for a decadently sweet version of classic rice pudding.

Yield	**6 cups**
Serving Size	**1 cup**
Prep Time	**15 minutes**
Cook Time	**2½ to 3½ hours**

¾ cup arborio rice

3 cups milk

1½ cups sugar

1¼ tsp. salt

1 large egg

6 TB. butter, diced

½ cup heavy cream

1. In a 3- or 4-quart (3- to 4-liter) slow cooker, place arborio rice.

2. In a medium bowl, whisk together milk, ½ cup sugar, ¼ teaspoon salt, and egg. Pour over rice.

3. Cover and cook on high for 2½ to 3½ hours or until rice is cooked through and most of liquids are absorbed, leaving a creamy sauce.

4. In a small saucepan over medium heat, combine remaining 1 cup sugar and butter. Cook, stirring constantly, for 3 to 5 minutes or until butter and sugar are melted and take on a golden color.

5. Slowly pour in heavy cream, bring to a boil, and simmer for 2 minutes. Remove from heat, and stir in remaining 1 teaspoon salt.

6. Stir half of salted caramel sauce into cooked rice pudding.

7. Serve hot, with remaining caramel drizzled over top.

Variation: If you don't have time to make your own caramel sauce, you can use a jar of caramel ice cream topping instead.

Traditional rice pudding is made with vanilla extract, a little butter, raisins, and either long- or short-grain white rice. Arborio rice holds up well in slow cooking and produces a hearty rice pudding. It also has a natural creaminess, thanks to its additional starch, that enriches the pudding's creamy texture.

Buttery croissants are soaked in a vanilla custard sprinkled with chunks of white chocolate in this ultradecadent bread pudding.

Yield	8 slices
Serving Size	1 slice
Prep Time	5 minutes
Cook Time	4 to 6 hours

6 large croissants

2 cups white chocolate chips

8 large eggs

2 cups milk

2 cups heavy cream

2/3 cup sugar

1 tsp. vanilla extract

1. Line a 6- to 8-quart (5.5- to 7.5-liter) slow cooker with parchment paper.

2. Tear croissants into bite-size pieces, and place them in the slow cooker.

3. Sprinkle white chocolate chips over croissants.

4. In a large bowl, and using a whisk, beat eggs until well combined.

5. Whisk in milk, heavy cream, sugar, and vanilla extract, and pour mixture over bread.

6. Cover and cook on high for 4 hours or on low for 6 hours.

7. Slice into 8 slices and serve warm.

Variation: For **Milk Chocolate Bread Pudding,** use milk chocolate chips in place of the white chocolate chips, and add 1/3 cup unsweetened cocoa powder with the sugar.

The kind of bread you use in a bread pudding affects the end result in both taste and texture. You can use French bread successfully as well as challah, brioche, and even sourdough.

White Chocolate Bread Pudding

Mile-High Chocolate Fudge Brownies

These brownies are thick and gooey for a fudgelike brownie that's worthy of being devoured.

Yield	12 slices
Serving Size	1 slice
Prep Time	5 minutes
Cook Time	3 or 4 hours

1 cup butter, melted

2¼ cups sugar

4 large eggs

1¼ cups unsweetened cocoa powder

1 tsp. salt

1 tsp. baking powder

1 TB. vanilla extract

1½ cups all-purpose flour

1 cup milk chocolate chips

1. Line a 6- to 8-quart (5.5- to 7.5-liter) slow cooker with an aluminum foil barrier and parchment paper.

2. In a large bowl, and using a large rubber spatula, combine butter and sugar.

3. Using an electric mixer on medium speed, mix in eggs.

4. Reduce the mixer speed to low, and mix in cocoa powder, salt, baking powder, and vanilla extract.

5. Using the spatula again, stir in all-purpose flour and milk chocolate chips until combined. Pour batter into the slow cooker.

6. Cover and cook on high for 3 or 4 hours or until middle of brownies no longer jiggle.

7. Remove brownies from the slow cooker, and cool on a wire rack before slicing.

It can be difficult to tell when brownies, breads, and other desserts are finished in the slow cooker because the center often remains shiny and appears to be uncooked. The best way to test for doneness is to tug on the parchment liner to see if the middle jiggles. You'll be able to tell if the center is still raw and in a liquid state.

The traditional elements of campfire s'mores are layered into a rich fudge brownie topped with puffy marshmallows.

Yield	12 slices
Serving Size	1 slice
Prep Time	10 minutes
Cook Time	3 or 4 hours

½ cup butter, melted

1 cup sugar

2 large eggs

½ cup unsweetened cocoa powder

½ tsp. salt

½ tsp. baking powder

1½ tsp. vanilla extract

¾ cup all-purpose flour

4 (5x2½-in.; 12x5.6cm) graham crackers

3 (1.5-oz.; 40g) milk chocolate candy bars

3 cups mini marshmallows

1. Line a 6- to 8-quart (5.5- to 7.5-liter) slow cooker with an aluminum foil barrier and parchment paper.

2. In a large bowl, and using a large rubber spatula, combine butter and sugar.

3. Using an electric mixer on medium speed, mix in eggs.

4. Reduce the mixer speed to low, and mix in cocoa powder, salt, baking powder, and vanilla extract.

5. Using the spatula again, stir in all-purpose flour.

6. Pour half of batter into the slow cooker.

7. Create a single layer of graham cracker on top of batter, breaking crackers to fit as needed.

8. Break chocolate candy bars into pieces and scatter in a single layer on top of graham crackers.

9. Stir 1 cup mini marshmallows into remaining brownie batter and pour over top of chocolate candy bars.

10. Cover and cook on high for 3 or 4 hours or until middle of brownies no longer jiggle.

11. Sprinkle remaining 2 cups mini marshmallows over cooked brownies.

12. Remove brownies from the slow cooker and cool on a wire rack before slicing.

The marshmallows are added in two spots because they liquefy when heated. The first cup melts and adds sweetness to the top brownie layer, and the remaining 2 cups stay mostly intact on top.

S'mores Brownies

Peanut Butter Fudge Cake

A soft and gooey peanut butter cake sits atop a hot fudge layer of chocolate goodness in this ultraindulgent dessert, perfect for lovers of chocolate and peanut butter.

Yield	6 cups
Serving Size	¾ cup
Prep Time	5 minutes
Cook Time	2 or 3 hours

1 cup all-purpose flour

1 cup sugar

½ cup creamy peanut butter

1 tsp. baking soda

½ tsp. baking powder

½ tsp. salt

½ cup buttermilk

½ cup water

2 TB. vegetable oil

1 tsp. vanilla extract

1 cup milk or semisweet chocolate chips

½ cup brown sugar, firmly packed

¼ cup unsweetened cocoa powder

1¼ cups boiling water

1. In a large bowl, combine all-purpose flour, sugar, peanut butter, baking soda, baking powder, salt, buttermilk, water, vegetable oil, and vanilla extract. Pour mixture into a 6- to 8-quart (5.5- to 7.5-liter) slow cooker.

2. Sprinkle milk chocolate chips, brown sugar, and cocoa powder over top of batter.

3. Pour boiling water over cake batter. Do not stir.

4. Cover and cook on high for 2 or 3 hours.

5. Serve warm.

This cake is assembled with the peanut butter cake on bottom and the fudge layer on top, but the layers reverse during cooking!

Gooey, rich, and *decadent* hardly begin to describe this magnificent chocolate dessert. Serve with a scoop of vanilla ice cream for an indulgent hot and cold dessert.

Yield	6 cups
Serving Size	¾ cup
Prep Time	5 minutes
Cook Time	2 or 3 hours

1 cup all-purpose flour

1 cup sugar

¾ cup unsweetened cocoa powder

1 tsp. baking soda

½ tsp. baking powder

½ tsp. salt

½ cup buttermilk

½ cup water

2 TB. vegetable oil

1 tsp. vanilla extract

1 cup milk or semisweet chocolate chips

¾ cup brown sugar, firmly packed

1½ cups hot water

1. In a large bowl, combine all-purpose flour, sugar, ½ cup cocoa powder, baking soda, baking powder, salt, buttermilk, water, vegetable oil, and vanilla extract. Pour batter into a 6- to 8-quart (5.5- to 7.5-liter) slow cooker.

2. Sprinkle milk chocolate chips, brown sugar, and remaining ¼ cup cocoa powder over top of cake batter.

3. Pour hot water over cake. Do not stir.

4. Cover and cook on high for 2 or 3 hours.

5. Serve warm.

This recipe produces a very gooey cake. As the cake cools, it will begin to firm. You can eat this dessert cooled, but it's best served warm.

Chocolate Mud Cake

Almond Poppy Seed Cake

The sweet flavor of almond and poppy seeds combine in a traditional white cake for a lusciously sweet and nutty dessert.

Yield	12 slices
Serving Size	1 slice
Prep Time	30 minutes
Cook Time	8 hours

2½ cups all-purpose flour

2 cups sugar

1 tsp. baking powder

½ tsp. baking soda

1⅓ cups buttermilk

½ cup butter, melted

1 tsp. almond extract

2 large eggs

1 TB. poppy seeds

1. Line a 6- to 8-quart (5.5- to 7.5-liter) slow cooker with an aluminum foil barrier and parchment paper.

2. In a large bowl, combine all-purpose flour, sugar, baking powder, and baking soda.

3. Pour in buttermilk, melted butter, almond extract, eggs, and poppy seeds, and whisk until smooth.

4. Pour batter in the prepared slow cooker.

5. Cover and cook on high for 3 or 4 hours or until center of cake is set.

6. Remove cake from the slow cooker and cool on a wire rack before slicing.

Variation: For **Lemon Poppy Seed Cake,** replace the almond extract with lemon extract. For plain **White Cake,** replace the almond extract with vanilla extract and omit the poppy seeds.

This cake is sweet enough that it doesn't require any frosting, but a simple glaze can be a nice aesthetic touch. In a small bowl, whisk together 1½ cups confectioners' sugar with 2 tablespoons milk. Add more milk as necessary to achieve the consistency you want. Allow the cake to cool completely before pouring glaze over the top.

The subtle citrus flavor of lemon brightens this sweet and dense cake. The slow cooker keeps the cake extra moist for a perfect pound cake.

Yield	12 slices
Serving Size	1 slice
Prep Time	5 minutes
Cook Time	3 hours

3 cups all-purpose flour

3 cups sugar

½ tsp. salt

¼ tsp. baking soda

1 cup butter, softened

6 large eggs

1 cup buttermilk

1 tsp. lemon extract

1 tsp. vanilla extract

2 TB. lemon zest

1. Line a 6- to 8-quart (5.5- to 7.5-liter) slow cooker with an aluminum foil barrier and parchment paper.

2. In a large bowl, combine all-purpose flour, sugar, salt, and baking soda.

3. Using an electric mixer on medium speed, whip butter into flour mixture.

4. Mix in eggs, buttermilk, lemon extract, vanilla extract, and lemon zest until smooth.

5. Pour batter into the prepared slow cooker.

6. Cover and cook on high for 3 hours or until cake is set.

7. Remove cake from the slow cooker and cool on a wire rack before slicing.

Variation: For **Orange Pound Cake,** use orange extract in place of lemon extract and orange zest in place of lemon zest. You also can dust the top of the cooled cake with confectioners' sugar before slicing.

Slicing a slow cooker cake can be a bit tricky, particularly if you're using an oval-shape cooker. For presentation purposes, you can square off the cake first and then cut it as you would a traditional cake. Or simply enjoy the rounded sides.

Lemon Pound Cake

Strawberry Swirl Cheesecakes

Silky cheesecake has never been easier than these individual-size cakes complete with graham cracker crusts and a sweet strawberry swirl.

Yield	5 cheesecakes
Serving Size	1 cheesecake
Prep Time	10 minutes
Cook Time	2 hours

1 cup crushed graham crackers

3 TB. butter, melted

2 (8-oz.; 225g) pkg. cream cheese, softened

¾ cup sugar

⅓ cup milk

2 large eggs

½ cup sour cream

1½ tsp. vanilla extract

2 TB. all-purpose flour

5 tsp. strawberry jam

1. In a small bowl, combine graham cracker crumbs and butter. Evenly divide crust mixture among 5 (½-pint; 8-ounce; 225-milliliter) wide-mouth jars, and press down firmly to form a crust.

2. In a large bowl, and using an electric mixer on medium speed, beat together cream cheese, sugar, milk, eggs, sour cream, vanilla extract, and all-purpose flour until smooth.

3. Divide batter among the jars, filling them to just below the rim. Cheesecakes will puff up slightly as they cook.

4. Place 1 teaspoon strawberry jam on top of each cake, and use a toothpick or butter knife to swirl jam gently on top of batter.

5. Place the jars in a 6- to 8-quart (5.5- to 7.5-liter) oval slow cooker. Carefully pour water around the jars to cover the bottom of the slow cooker with 1 inch (2.5 centimeters) water.

6. Cover and cook on high for 2 hours.

7. Remove the jars from the slow cooker and cool on a wire rack. Cover and store in the refrigerator until ready to serve.

Variation: You can use any flavor of jam for mix-and-match variety.

This recipe demonstrates how the slow cooker can work as a miniature oven, baking individual cakes in their own pans. Any oven-safe dish that fits into your slow cooker, including ramekins, springform pans, or even pie plates, would work.

These dessert bars will be a fast favorite at any party where you serve them, with their layers of gooey caramel and melted chocolate sandwiched between soft oatmeal-cookie layers.

Yield	12 bars
Serving Size	1 bar
Prep Time	5 minutes
Cook Time	2 or 3 hours

2 cups all-purpose flour

2 cups quick oats

1½ cups brown sugar, firmly packed

1 tsp. baking soda

½ tsp. salt

1 cup butter, melted

2 cups semisweet chocolate chips

1 (12-oz.; 340g) jar caramel ice cream topping

1. Line a 6- to 8-quart (5.5- to 7.5-liter) slow cooker with parchment paper.

2. In a large bowl, combine all-purpose flour, quick oats, brown sugar, baking soda, and salt.

3. Pour in melted butter and stir to form a crumbly oat mixture. Pour half of oat mixture into the bottom of the prepared slow cooker, and press down to form a smooth crust.

4. Sprinkle semisweet chocolate chips evenly over bottom crust.

5. Pour caramel ice cream topping over chocolate chips.

6. Pour remaining oat mixture over caramel and press down gently to form a smooth top crust.

7. Cover and cook on high for 2 or 3 hours.

8. Remove caramelitas from the slow cooker and cool on a wire rack before slicing.

Variation: Add ½ cup chopped walnuts over the caramel layer for a nutty touch.

Lining the slow cooker with parchment paper is a key step in this recipe because it enables you to easily remove the bars from the slow cooker. While hot, the bars will be unstable, but they'll set as they cool. These bars are delicious when eaten hot with a spoon, but they can't be cut into bars until after they're completely cooled.

Caramelitas

Glossary

all-purpose flour Flour that contains only the inner part of the wheat grain. It's suitable for everything from cakes to gravies.

allspice A spice named for its flavor echoes of several spices such as cinnamon, cloves, and nutmeg.

arborio rice A plump Italian rice often used for risotto.

artichoke heart The center of the artichoke flower, often sold canned or frozen.

arugula A spicy-peppery green that has a sharp, distinctive flavor.

baking powder A dry ingredient used to increase volume and lighten or leaven baked goods.

balsamic vinegar A heavy, dark, sweet vinegar produced primarily in Italy from a specific type of grape and aged in wood barrels.

basil A flavorful, almost sweet, resinous herb delicious with tomatoes and used in many Italian- and Mediterranean-style dishes.

beat To quickly mix substances.

blanch To place a food in boiling water for about 1 minute or less to partially cook and then douse with cool water to halt the cooking.

blend To completely mix something, usually with a blender or food processor, slower than beating.

boil To heat a liquid to the point where water is forced to turn into steam, causing the liquid to bubble.

bouillon Dried essence of stock from chicken, beef, vegetables, or other ingredients.

braise To cook with the introduction of a liquid, usually over a period of time.

broil To cook in a dry oven under the overhead high-heat element.

broth See stock.

brown To cook in a skillet, turning, until the food's surface is seared and brown in color, to lock in the juices.

brown rice A nutritious whole-grain rice, including the germ, with a pale brown or tan color.

bulgur A wheat kernel that's been steamed, dried, and crushed.

caramelize To cook vegetables or meat in butter or oil over low heat until they soften, sweeten, and develop a caramel color. Also to cook sugar over low heat until it develops a sweet caramel flavor.

caraway A spicy seed used for bread, pork, cheese, and cabbage dishes. It's known to reduce stomach upset.

cardamom An intense, sweet-smelling spice used in baking and coffee and common in Indian cooking.

cayenne A fiery spice made from hot chile peppers, especially the slender, red, very hot cayenne.

chickpea (or garbanzo bean) A roundish, golden bean high in fiber and low in fat, often used as the base ingredient in hummus.

chile (or chili) A term for a number of hot peppers, ranging from the relatively mild ancho to the blisteringly hot habanero.

chili powder A warm, rich seasoning blend that includes chile pepper, cumin, garlic, and oregano.

chive A herb that grows in bunches of long leaves and offers a light onion flavor.

chop To cut into pieces, usually qualified such as "*coarsely chopped*" or with a size measurement such as "chopped into ½-inch (1.25cm) pieces." "Finely chopped" is much closer to mince.

chutney A thick condiment often served with Indian curries made with fruits and/or vegetables with vinegar, sugar, and spices.

cilantro A member of the parsley family often used in Mexican dishes. The seed is called coriander in North America; elsewhere, the plant is called coriander.

cinnamon A rich, aromatic spice commonly used in baking or desserts.

clove A sweet, strong, almost wintergreen-flavor spice used in baking.

coriander A rich, warm, spicy seed used in all types of recipes.

cornstarch A thickener made from the refined starch of a corn kernel's endosperm. Before it's added to a recipe, it's often mixed with a liquid to make a paste and avoid clumps.

cream To beat a fat such as butter, often with another ingredient such as sugar, to soften and aerate a batter.

cumin A fiery, smoky-tasting spice popular in Middle Eastern and Indian dishes. It's most often used ground.

curry Rich, spicy, Indian-style sauces and the dishes prepared with them. Curry powder is the base seasoning.

curry powder A ground blend of rich and flavorful spices such as hot pepper, nutmeg, cumin, cinnamon, pepper, and turmeric.

custard A cooked mixture of eggs and milk popular as a base for desserts.

dash A few drops, usually of a liquid, released by a quick shake.

deglaze To scrape up bits of meat and seasoning left in a pan or skillet after cooking, usually by adding a liquid such as wine or broth and creating a flavorful stock.

dice To cut into small cubes about ¼-inch (6.5mm) square.

Dijon mustard A hearty, spicy mustard made in the style of the Dijon region of France.

dill A herb perfect for eggs, salmon, cheese dishes, and vegetables.

dredge To coat a piece of food on all sides with a dry substance such as flour or cornmeal.

extra-virgin olive oil See olive oil.

falafel A Middle Eastern food made of seasoned, ground chickpeas formed into balls, cooked, and often used as a filling in pitas.

fennel In seed form, a fragrant, licorice-tasting herb. The bulbs have a mild flavor and a celery-like crunch.

flour Grains ground into a meal. Wheat is perhaps the most common flour, but oats, rye, buckwheat, soybeans, chickpeas, and others are also used.

fold To combine a dense and a light mixture with a gentle move from the middle of the bowl outward to preserve the mixture's airy nature.

frittata An egg dish that's cooked slowly, without stirring, in a skillet and then either flipped or finished under the broiler.

fry See sauté.

garlic A pungent and flavorful member of the onion family. A garlic bulb contains multiple cloves; each clove, when chopped, yields about 1 teaspoon garlic.

ginger A flavorful root available fresh or dried and ground that adds a pungent, sweet, and spicy quality to a dish.

Greek yogurt A strained yogurt that's a good natural source of protein, calcium, and probiotics.

hearts of palm Firm, elongated, off-white cylinders from the inside of a palm tree stem tip.

herbes de Provence A seasoning mix of basil, fennel, marjoram, rosemary, sage, and thyme, common in the south of France.

hoisin sauce A sweet Asian condiment similar to ketchup made with soybeans, sesame, chile peppers, and sugar.

horseradish A sharp, spicy root. Use sparingly.

hummus A thick, Middle Eastern spread made of puréed chickpeas, lemon juice, olive oil, garlic, and often tahini.

Italian seasoning A blend of dried herbs, including basil, oregano, rosemary, and thyme.

julienne A French word meaning "to slice into very thin pieces."

kalamata olive Traditionally from Greece, a medium-small, long black olive with a rich, smoky flavor.

Key lime A very small lime grown primarily in Florida known for its tart taste.

knead To work dough, often with your hands, to make it pliable. Kneading is fundamental in the process of making yeast breads.

kosher salt A coarse-grained salt made without any additives or iodine.

lentil A tiny lens-shape pulse used in European, Middle Eastern, and Indian cuisines.

marinate To soak a food in a seasoned sauce to impart flavor and make tender, as with meat.

marjoram A sweet herb similar to oregano popular in Greek, Spanish, and Italian dishes.

mince To cut into very small pieces, smaller than diced, about ⅛ inch (3.18mm) or smaller.

nutmeg A sweet, fragrant, musky spice used primarily in baking.

olive The green or black fruit of the olive tree.

olive oil A fragrant liquid produced by crushing or pressing olives. Extra-virgin olive oil, the most flavorful and highest quality, is produced from the olives' first pressing; oil is also produced from later pressings.

oregano A fragrant, slightly astringent herb used often in Greek, Spanish, and Italian dishes.

orzo A rice-shape pasta used in Greek cooking.

oxidation The gradual browning of a fruit or vegetable from exposure to air. Minimize oxidation by rubbing cut surfaces with lemon juice.

paella A Spanish dish of rice, shellfish, onion, meats, rich broth, and herbs.

paprika A rich, red, warm, earthy spice that lends a rich red color to many dishes.

parsley A fresh-tasting green leafy herb, often used as a garnish.

pesto A thick spread or sauce made with pine nuts, fresh basil, garlic, olive oil, and Parmesan cheese.

pilaf A savory rice dish in which the rice is browned in butter or oil and then cooked in a flavorful liquid such as a broth.

pine nut A rich (high in fat), flavorful, nut traditionally used in pesto.

poach To cook a food in simmering liquid such as water, wine, or broth.

polenta A cornmeal mush that can be eaten hot with butter or cooked until firm and cut into squares.

portobello mushroom A large, brown, chewy, flavorful mushroom.

purée To reduce a food to a thick, creamy texture, typically using a blender or food processor.

quinoa A nutty-flavored seed high in protein and calcium.

reduce To boil or simmer a broth or sauce to remove some of the water content and yield a more concentrated flavor.

risotto A creamy Italian rice dish made by browning arborio rice in butter or oil and slowly adding liquid to cook the rice.

roast To cook food uncovered in an oven, usually without additional liquid.

rosemary A pungent, sweet herb used with chicken, pork, fish, and especially lamb.

roux A mixture of butter or another fat and flour used to thicken sauces and soups.

saffron A yellow, flavorful spice made from the stamens of crocus flowers.

sage An herb with a slightly musty, fruity, lemon-rind scent and sunny flavor.

sauté To pan-cook over lower heat than what's used for frying.

savory A popular herb with a fresh, woody taste. *Savory* can also describe the flavor of food.

sear To quickly brown the exterior of a food, especially meat, over high heat.

sesame oil An oil made from pressing sesame seeds. It's tasteless if clear and aromatic and flavorful if brown.

shallot A member of the onion family that grows in a bulb somewhat like garlic but has a milder onion flavor.

short-grain rice A starchy rice that clumps easily.

simmer To boil a liquid gently so it barely bubbles.

skillet (also frying pan) A flat-bottomed metal pan with a handle designed to cook food on a stovetop.

skim To remove fat or other material from the top of liquid.

steam To suspend a food over boiling water and allow the heat of the steam to cook the food.

stew To slowly cook pieces of food submerged in a liquid. Also a dish prepared using this method.

stir-fry To cook small pieces of food in a wok or skillet over high heat, moving and turning the food quickly to cook all sides.

stock A flavorful broth made by cooking meats and/or vegetables with seasonings until the liquid absorbs these flavors. The liquid is strained, and the solids are discarded. Stock can be eaten alone or used as a base for soups, stews, etc.

tapenade A thick, chunky spread made from savory ingredients such as olives, lemon juice, and anchovies.

tarragon A sweet, rich-smelling herb perfect with vegetables, seafood, chicken, and pork.

teriyaki A Japanese-style sauce made of soy sauce, rice wine, ginger, and sugar.

thyme A minty, zesty herb.

turmeric A spicy, pungent yellow root. It's the source of the yellow color in many mustards.

tzatziki A Greek dip traditionally made with Greek yogurt, cucumbers, garlic, and mint.

vinegar An acidic liquid often made from fermented grapes, apples, or rice and used as a dressing and seasoning.

water chestnut A white, crunchy, juicy tuber popular in many Asian dishes.

whisk To rapidly mix, introducing air to the mixture.

white vinegar Vinegar produced from grain.

whole grain A grain derived from the seeds of grasses such as wheat, oats, rye, barley, buckwheat, corn, or rice.

whole-wheat flour Wheat flour that contains the entire grain.

wild rice A grass, often considered a rice, that has a rich, nutty flavor.

yeast Tiny fungi that, when mixed with water, sugar, flour, and heat, release carbon dioxide bubbles that cause bread to rise.

zest Small slivers of peel, usually from citrus fruit.

Index

C

D

E

F

G

N–O

P

Q–R